Avoid Dialysis Diet Plan for Kidney Disease

A research-based guide for 50+ CKD patients on what to eat and avoid while on a renal diet.

By
Janeth Kingston BSN, RN

From The Author

Hello and thank you for investing in your health with **"Avoid Dialysis Diet Plan for Kidney Disease"** I'm deeply grateful for your trust, and I'm excited to be part of your journey towards better kidney health.

My name is Janeth Kingston, BSN, RN. I have spent over a decade working as a dedicated nephrology nurse, both in the US and the EU. Throughout my career, I've been privileged to contribute to the research and development that improves the quality of life for those living with Stage 3 to 5 Chronic Kidney Disease (CKD).

This book is the culmination of years of research, patient interaction, and careful study. This book uses the same research-based background from a project we have undertaken together with numerous nephrology experts. The project has been recognized and awarded by esteemed bodies like the American Society of Nephrology, which awarded our work in their KidneyX program in 2019. You can check their website www.KidneyX.org under "Digitally Delivered Behavior Change Program to Help Patients Delay Dialysis". The success of our program has also been presented at prestigious nephrology conferences, such as Kidney Week in Washington DC and the ERA-EDTA in Europe.

Since 2017, my team and I have helped over 10,589 CKD patients navigate their dietary needs and confidently manage their condition. Each of these individual stories has further enriched our knowledge and understanding, and I'm thrilled to bring that collective wisdom to you today.

In collaboration with seasoned nephrology researchers, kidney-specialized chefs, and leading nephrologists, we have created this guide. Our goal? To provide you with a simple, accessible roadmap to managing your condition and avoiding dialysis.

As you take your first steps on this journey, remember: change is a process, not a destination. Be patient with yourself and take each day as it comes. With each page you turn, you're taking a proactive step towards better health.

I'd like to extend an invitation to ***join our FREE weekly newsletter online***, where we share:

- weekly kidney-safe recipes
- meal plans, and
- the latest research-based advice.

Follow these steps to join our online weekly newsletter:

1. Please type on your phone or pc browser **https://go.renaltracker.com/joinnewsletter** to sign up.
2. Or you can also scan the QR code below.
   a. Open your phone's camera
   b. Hover your phone over the QR code
   c. Tap on the link and enter your name and email.

It's a great way to stay informed and feel supported as you navigate your CKD journey.

Once again, thank you for your trust. Here's to a healthier, brighter future for your kidneys.

With gratitude,

Janeth Kingston, BSN, RN

Table of Contents

INTRODUCTION

The Need for a CKD-Specific Diet

Taking charge of your own health can help you achieve better outcomes. This can also give you a sense of empowerment and, eventually, give you the motivation you need to be responsible with the choices you make concerning your health.

And one simple way to do this is to take an active role in your health decisions, particularly on things you can control on your own: Your Diet.

Changing your diet will require a tremendous shift in your routines. You'll need to avoid most of your favorite meals. You'll need to fit in types of food you're not particularly fond of in your diet plan. You'll also need to make changes in your grocery lists, most especially in your budget since healthy eating can quite get financially demanding. And the list goes on.

But if you were to take the right steps towards this change, it will remarkably improve your health outcomes and alter your overall lifestyle to a better one. And I assure you that throughout your journey to a better kidney health, it will be worth it.

Now, I know that change, especially when you have to replace bad habits with good ones, can be hard and may take time and patience. But if you keep practicing and stick with your new choices, **it will become part of your daily routine.**

That is why I'd like to lay a solid foundation before we get started with anything, and really pound things at the beginning of this book.

From setting your goals to getting support, it will require several steps to get to where you should be. But one of the most important steps is to **figure out what your barriers are.** By identifying your barriers and having a plan to help you get past them will help you change bad habits into good habits.

Overcoming Your Barriers To Healthy Eating

What's a barrier?

A barrier is anything that causes you to slip up in your goal to make the lifestyle changes you need, such as changing your eating habits. By figuring out what those barriers are and how you can get around them can help you reach your kidney-friendly eating goals. When you hit a certain barrier, get support, especially from your family, friends, or even your kidney doctor.

Having slip ups is normal. Chef Duane Sunwold, a dear friend turned CKD chef, once battled hard with his own Chronic Kidney Disease. In fact, the first time he was advised to change his diet by completely taking out animal protein, he slipped up and decided to eat a cheeseburger instead! But when he was committed to his goal, he managed to feel much better and improved his creatinine levels from 4.99 to 0.8! Therefore, you need to have a plan on how to get back on track for when that happens.

So, what's the best way to overcome barriers? You have to identify them ahead of time and create a backup plan on how to deal with them. There will be some barriers right away, that will keep you from trying to change a habit, while others may appear later on. When they do, get support by talking to your family and friends who are there to cheer you on. And if you have any questions or concerns about your health, talk to your doctor to make sure you're on the right track.

There are a few reasons why you will have trouble changing your eating habits. Here are some of them and how to handle each one.

"I'll never be able to change how I eat."

By not believing you are capable of doing something, especially change, is often **just a fear of failure.** This kind of barrier can keep you from even starting to make a lifestyle change. Here are two possible solutions:

1. Carefully define "success" and "failure". If your goal is to lower your nutrient intake, like Sodium, from 2,000mg to 1,200mg a day, you will probably be successful. But if your goal is to cure kidney disease or eat perfectly, it is not realistic and may lead to failure.
2. Set small, yet measurable goals. Eating a low-sodium fruit is an easy goal to reach. However, completely giving up your favorite foods is much harder, and you will be more likely to not try.

"I don't have time to make changes."

This is a very common reason not to change. It can take in the form of *"My life is just too busy right now"*, or *"I have more important things to do"*, or *"I will start next week"*. Here are four possible solutions:

1. Manage your time better. Find time-management techniques that will work best for you.
2. Ask others how they manage to fit good nutrition into their lives.
3. Don't try to make too many changes at the same time. Small changes take less time, but they add. Remember, small changes eventually add up to huge results.
4. Ask for help from family and friends when you change your eating habits.

"I don't like healthy foods"

Most people use this reason and may come in the form of, *"I don't like vegetables"*, *"I don't like low-fat foods"*, or *"I'll miss eating them"*. Here are two possible solutions:

1. Be patient and give it time. Food preferences are not easy at first, but they do change over time. Remember when you start changing by picking one habit at time, it will eventually become part of your routine. Decide to withhold your judgements about what you like or dislike in foods until you have given the new foods a chance. If you need help, be sure to discuss with your doctor and dietitian how to integrate foods into your new kidney diet.
2. Take it slow. You don't have to completely give up your favorite foods, but you may have to change how often and how much you eat them. Make your changes small, and give yourself time to adjust your diet.

"Healthy foods cost too much."

It's true that food items such as fresh produce, whole-grain breads, and other healthy food items can cost you more than purchasing cheap fast food or quick meals. Sometimes it makes you think that maybe you should just go with cheap fast food every day. But you can stay within your budget if you carefully plan your meals, know what to buy, and what to cook. The more time you invest, the more money you'll be able to save. Here's are possible solutions:

1. Save money by learning and planning. To carefully plan a week's worth of meals at a time, be sure to consult your dietitian for a meal plan that best fits your condition. This is so you are not likely to go out to eat on the spur of the moment.

2. When you're at the grocery store, save money by buying store brands instead of name brands and do shopping in bulk foods aisle.

3. If you're not used to preparing and cooking your own meals, you have to start learning.

"I'm not good at making changes."

This one actually may take the form of *"I'm too old to make changes."* Often, low self-esteem makes it hard to change. Here are possible solutions:

1. Make small and measurable changes. They are easier to make and monitor. For example, try eating a low-sodium fruit instead of the usual fruit.

2. Work on your self-esteem *(if this is an issue for you)*. Seeking help from a counselor can help with issues of self-esteem. The success that you will feel from improving your eating habits may improve your self-esteem as well. Little

by little, you may begin to change the way you view yourself and your ability to change.

To help you identify your own barriers, think about the last few times you thought about changing your eating habits but didn't follow through with it.

What stopped you from doing it? Be sure to write your reasons. For each reason, write a response that will help you reconsider your choice. After which, look at your list of reasons and responses whenever you are about to make a choice on what to eat.

Why should you start small? Because...

"Success is the sum of all small efforts, repeated day in and day out" - R. Collier

The Role of Diet in CKD Progression

Now that you have gone through your need of a CKD-specific diet and identified personal areas that might keep you from achieving your goals for health, let's dive a little deeper on why diet is so important in the management of Chronic Kidney Disease and to keep it from progressing.

"Diet is one of the largest modifiable risk factors for chronic kidney disease (CKD)-related death and disability" Snelson et. *al.* While it is no longer a mystery that certain types of food have been linked to the development of CKD, studies have also shown that optimized diets which include both restrictions and modifications of certain nutrients and minerals in the food that we eat help in reducing the burden of CKD.

These restrictions and modifications focus on specific micro and macronutrients such as Protein, Sodium, Potassium, and Phosphorus, as well as the intake of dietary fibers, and certain carbohydrates, and even go as intensive as involving the food preparation process to ensure that the patient only gets the preventative benefits from his/her diet.

How This Book Can Help

This is not another recipe book where you will find suggestions for your next meal. *(But I'll sure to indulge you in some recipes as we move along).* In the next few chapters, you will discover in-depth but practically applicable knowledge on how you can take an even better approach to managing your kidney disease.

From understanding the connection of diet and how it works in CKD, to learning by heart the ins and outs of nutritional modification, to handling special occasions and creating a holistically balanced wellness involving your mind and body, through exercise and stress management.

However, if you are reading this for a family or friend, this book will equip you with the right knowledge to effectively assist your loved ones and even pass the knowledge forward to whoever might need it in the future.

This book is written based on recent research and personal experiences of working with CKD Patients for the past 10 years. Thus, I too am convinced, that this book will help you in battling with CKD as with everyone who are with you in this journey.

Understanding CKD

Before we take that plunge into the amazing world of CKD management through diet, let's first do a quick recap of what this is we are dealing with in the first place.

Knowing Your CKD Stage.

You might have heard a couple dozen times, that CKD management does not come in a one-size-fits-all solution, and rightly so due to the diversity of the factors that need to be considered e.g. age, weight, lifestyle, and so on. But one thing that makes the deal here is when you understand your diagnosis to the nines, so you have a better grasp in making informed decisions about your health. Let's get to know YOU a little better, so we can both begin this journey already knowing important things for your CKD Stage.

What CKD Stage are you diagnosed in?

_____

So here's what you need to know:

An eGFR between 30 and 59 ml/min indicates that there's some damage to the kidneys and they; are not working as well as they should. As a result, you are more likely to have health complications such as high blood pressure, anemia, and bone disease.

But did you know that Stage 3 is divided into 2 stages?

Stage 3a means that you have an eGFR between 45-59 ml/min, while stage 3b means that you have an eGFR between 30 and 44 ml/min.

Symptoms might be already present at this stage, such as:

- Fatigue
- Fluid retention, swelling (edema) of extremities and shortness of breath:
- Urination changes (foamy; dark orange, brown, tea-colored or red if it contains blood; and urinating more or less than normal)
- Kidney pain felt in your back - Sleep problems due to muscle cramps or restless legs

To keep your kidneys from getting worse, you need to switch to a kidney-friendly diet that consists of:

- Limiting your nutrient intake such as sodium, protein, phosphorus, potassium, and calcium.
- Consuming some grains, fruits and vegetables (potassium and phosphorus are at normal levels).
- Cutting back carbohydrates (if you have diabetes).
- Decreasing saturated fats to help lower cholesterol.
- Take in prescribed medication from your doctor.

Disease Progression and Options

Now, as the CKD progresses, here are the following symptoms that are usually experienced at stage 4:

- Fatigue
- Fluid retention
- Urination changes (foamy; dark orange, brown, tea-colored or red if it contains blood; and urinating more or less than normal)
- Kidney pain felt in your back
- Sleep problems due to muscle cramps or restless legs
- Nausea
- Metallic taste in mouth

- Loss of appetite
- Numbness or tingling in the toes or fingers

Also known as **End Stage Kidney Disease (ESKD)**, the kidneys have already lost their ability to do their job effectively and treatment options such as hemodialysis, peritoneal dialysis, or kidney transplantation is needed to live.

Once you begin your treatment (depending on what you choose), your diet will continue to be a very big part of your treatment. Some of this would include:

- Including grains, fruits and vegetables, but limiting or avoiding whole grains and certain fruits and vegetables that are high in phosphorus or potassium
- A diet that is low in saturated fat and cholesterol and moderate in total fats, especially if cholesterol is high or if you have diabetes or heart disease
- Limiting intake of refined and processed foods high in sodium and prepare foods with less salt or high-sodium ingredients
- Limiting fluid intake

Now, I know what you're thinking…"It's a lot of information to take in." That is just a very quick run-through of what you are about to learn. Don't worry as I will break them down carefully for you in the coming chapters.

Importance of Early Intervention

When patients come to me, most of them feel they are alone in dealing with their kidney condition. They become so caught up in this belief that when you tell them how they can take action to manage their condition, it somehow reinforces that idea even more… And I understand that...

Because in the beginning, when the news was given to you, you likely found yourself in a state of shock.

Many kidney patients find it hard to believe that what the doctor is saying is true. It feels so unlikely, too overwhelming. It becomes difficult to comprehend what chronic kidney damage is, because not a lot of people talk about it like they do with diabetes or heart attack.

"No, it is not true, it will not be that bad", says your mind. This is a very normal defense mechanism: denial. But, the most important thing for you to know - in this moment - **is that taking proactive steps now may slow down your kidney disease.** Which is one of the reasons why you picked up this book, right? And as long as you're here, I'll show you the ropes little by little so that in due time, you'll be able **to learn how to do it yourself**

Studies have shown that **patients** who are actively engaged in their health and care experience better health outcomes. You can start with your lab test results. Which reminds me, have you had your lab tests done recently? Because if you have, you can use your new found knowledge to get a better picture of your overall health.

Your test results are a way **to assess the progression of your kidney condition**. For example, by keeping track of your serum creatinine or eGFR, you'll have a clearer idea of the state of your kidneys.

Now that makes it sound a bit intimidating, but trust me, it isn't hard to do once you know what to keep track of. And self-monitoring is one way to achieve that.

Okay, okay, what exactly is self-monitoring?

Self-monitoring emphasizes how YOU are part of your own healthcare team. In terms of your kidney health, self-monitoring means noting down two important categories:

1. **Your test results**, and,
2. **Your lifestyle**, which includes your diet and exercise habits, among others (we'll be talking more about these soon in the coming chapters!)

It's a simple solution, but it works. And the experts know it:

- Researchers agree that self-monitoring (or self-management) is associated with positive patient outcomes, and that fostering this behavior can **have long-term positive effects.**
- Patients in a self-monitoring program enjoyed more health benefits than those who didn't. This includes **fewer hospitalizations, feeling healthier, and being more active, among others.**
- Guidelines by psychologists include encouraging self-monitoring among chronic kidney disease patients, **to better help them accept and deal with their condition**.

Importance of Age-Based Diet

Age and Metabolism

While anybody can benefit from this book, I did mention that CKD management is diversified by many factors, and I have particularly paid close attention to the 50+ patients who I have had most experience with over the years.

Now, since diet has a direct relationship with your metabolism, let's talk about it for a while as it relates to age as well. Metabolism refers to all the physical and chemical processes in the body that convert or use energy, such as breathing, circulating blood, controlling body temperature, cell growth, brain and nerve function, and contraction of muscles. The rate at which these processes occur is known as metabolic rate.

There is a connection between age and metabolism. Here are some key points:

1 **Basal Metabolic Rate (BMR)**: Your BMR is the number of calories your body needs to perform basic functions, like breathing and digestion. As we age, our BMR generally decreases. This decrease is typically due to loss of lean body mass (muscle), which is metabolically active.

2 **Muscle Mass Decline**: As we age, we naturally lose muscle mass, a process known as sarcopenia. This process generally starts in our 30s and continues as we age, accelerating particularly after age 50. Because muscle tissue burns more calories than fat tissue, our metabolism slows as our muscle mass decreases.

3 **Physical Activity**: In general, physical activity decreases as people age. This decrease in activity contributes to a lower metabolic rate and can lead to weight gain if calorie intake isn't adjusted to match the lower energy expenditure.

4 **Hormonal Changes**: As we age, our bodies undergo various hormonal changes. In women, menopause causes significant hormonal changes that can slow metabolism. In men, testosterone levels slowly decrease, which can lead to a decrease in muscle mass and a slower metabolism.

5 **Cellular Aging**: At the cellular level, aging is associated with a decrease in the number of mitochondria, which are

the "powerhouses" of cells where metabolic processes occur. This decrease can also contribute to a slower metabolism.

In short, as we age, our metabolism tends to slow down due to factors like loss of muscle mass, decreased physical activity, hormonal changes, and cellular aging. However, lifestyle interventions such as regular physical exercise and maintaining a healthy diet can help counter the effects of aging on metabolism. Add a Chronic Kidney Disease diagnosis in the mix, you would all the more want your metabolism to be at its best, to get the optimum results on the dietary interventions that we will be putting into practice for your kidney health.

Nutritional Needs of the 50+ Age Group

Furthermore, our bodies also undergo various physiological changes that influence our nutritional needs. While calorie needs may decrease due to a slower metabolism and less physical activity, the need for certain nutrients may increase. Here is a guide to some of the nutritional needs for individuals aged 50 and above:

1. **Protein**: During aging, there's often a loss of muscle mass. To help counteract this, older adults might need more protein than their younger counterparts. The recommended dietary allowance (RDA) for protein is 46 grams per day for women and 56 grams per day for men.
2. **Fiber**: Fiber can help reduce the risk of heart disease and type 2 diabetes, which are more common in older adults. It can also help prevent constipation, a common problem in older people. Men over 50 should aim for 30 grams of fiber per day, and women should aim for 21 grams.

3. **Vitamins and Minerals:**

- Vitamin B12: With aging, some people lose the ability to absorb vitamin B12 from food. This vitamin is important for creating red blood cells and maintaining nerve function. People over 50 should get most of their vitamin B12 from fortified foods or dietary supplements.

- Calcium and Vitamin D: These are crucial for bone health. With age, the skin becomes less efficient at synthesizing vitamin D, and the kidneys are less able to convert it to its active form. Thus, older adults may need to get more of these nutrients through diet or supplements.

- Potassium: Increasing potassium intake along with reducing sodium (salt) may lower blood pressure and reduce the risk of developing kidney stones and bone loss.

4. **Hydration:** As we age, our sense of thirst may not be as sharp. This can lead to dehydration. It's important for older adults to drink water regularly, even if they don't feel thirsty.

5. **Healthy Fats**: Heart health becomes increasingly important as we age. Opting for healthy fats, such as those found in avocados, nuts, seeds, and fish, can help maintain heart health.

6. **Limited Sodium**: To help control blood pressure, it's recommended that adults over 50 limit their sodium intake to 2,300 mg per day.

That was quite a foretaste of the rich journey on CKD dieting that we will be embarking in the chapters of this book. See you in the next chapter as we begin to talk about the connection between CKD and food.

Chapter 1:
The CKD-Diet Connection

Chronic kidney disease (CKD) is a major public health burden, with a global prevalence of ~ 11% in the general adult population. If left untreated, CKD slowly progresses to end-stage renal disease, which requires dialysis or kidney transplant. CKD is bidirectionally associated with cardiovascular diseases (CVD). Hypertension and type 2 diabetes mellitus (T2DM) are independent risk factors for CKD, and their global prevalences are increasing, which will likely impact CKD. Worldwide, a 31.7% increase in CKD mortality was observed over the last decade.

What Does Food Do to Your Kidneys?

As you may have known by now, our kidneys are vital organs within our body, performing a plethora of tasks that help maintain equilibrium within our body. Among their significant roles is the processing of various nutrients from the food we consume. Allow me to bore you a bit with a quick review of how the kidneys manage different types of nutrients in our body, I promise you this will be significant later on:

Water

The kidneys play a crucial role in maintaining the body's water balance. After the body utilizes the necessary water for its various metabolic processes, the excess is eliminated through the kidneys as urine. This process is regulated by a hormone called antidiuretic hormone (ADH), which increases the water reabsorption in the kidneys, and aldosterone, which conserves sodium and eliminates potassium.

Electrolytes

Kidneys balance the levels of several important electrolytes in the body, including sodium, potassium, calcium, and phosphate. Sodium and potassium levels are particularly critical. For example, aldosterone, a hormone secreted by the adrenal glands, signals the kidneys to retain sodium and water and excrete potassium, thus helping to maintain electrolyte balance.

Proteins

Typically, proteins are not excreted in the urine because they are large molecules and cannot pass through the glomerulus during filtration. However, the kidneys do play a role in metabolizing proteins. They help to extract excess amino acids and other byproducts of protein metabolism (like urea) from the blood and excrete them in urine.

Carbohydrates

After carbohydrates are broken down into glucose in the digestive system, the kidneys help reabsorb glucose back into the bloodstream. The kidneys also have a minor role in gluconeogenesis - the production of new glucose.

Fats

The kidneys do not play a major role in processing fats. However, they can be affected by a high-fat diet, which can lead to kidney disease over time.

Vitamins and Minerals

The kidneys help maintain the balance of many vitamins and minerals in the body. For example, they help regulate levels of vitamin D and calcium - the kidneys convert vitamin D from supplements or the sun to its active form in the body, which helps regulate calcium and phosphate levels.

Please remember that this is a simplified overview. The actual processes involve complex biochemical and physiological mechanisms. It's also important to note that while kidneys are very efficient at their jobs, they can be damaged by poor nutrition, high blood pressure, diabetes, and other health conditions. Therefore, maintaining a healthy diet and lifestyle is crucial for kidney health.

The Impact of Overworking Your Kidneys

Now when we err to the side of being nonchalant about taking care of our kidney health by probably taking excessive protein, high sugar consumption, poor fluid intake just to name a few, we overwork our kidneys, also known as kidney overload which now leads to several adverse health effects, which collectively or on its own progress into Severe Kidney Damage, Chronic Kidney Disease, and worst End Stage Renal Disease:

Proteinuria

When kidneys are overworked, they may allow some proteins to pass through their filters into the urine, a condition known as proteinuria. This can be an early sign of kidney damage.

High Blood Pressure

The kidneys play a crucial role in regulating blood pressure by balancing fluid levels and releasing hormones that control blood pressure. Overworking kidneys can disrupt these processes, leading to high blood pressure, which can further damage the kidneys.

Electrolyte Imbalances

Kidneys are responsible for balancing various electrolytes in the body. Overworking the kidneys can lead to imbalances in electrolytes, such as potassium, calcium, and phosphate, which can affect multiple body functions.

Kidney Stones

Overworking the kidneys, especially due to high protein diets or dehydration, can lead to the formation of kidney stones. These are hard deposits of minerals and salts that form inside your kidneys.

Kidney Infections

Overworked kidneys may not effectively remove waste and toxins from the body, potentially leading to infections.

Edema

The kidneys also remove excess fluid from the body. If they are overworked and unable to efficiently perform this task, fluid can build up leading to edema (swelling), particularly in the legs, ankles, and feet.

Foods That Put Extra Strain on Your Kidneys

While some of the causes of kidney damage are linked to certain disease conditions, even these, at the very root can be traced back to food and nutrition. Certain foods can put extra strain on the kidneys, particularly when consumed in excess. These include:

High-Sodium Foods

Too much sodium can cause the kidneys to work harder and can also lead to high blood pressure, which can damage the kidneys over time. Processed foods tend to be especially high in sodium.

High-Protein Foods

While protein is an essential part of a balanced diet, eating excessive amounts of animal protein (like red meat) can strain the kidneys. This is because metabolizing protein produces a waste product called urea that the kidneys must filter out.

High-Potassium Foods

Kidneys help balance potassium levels in the body. If your kidneys are not functioning properly, consuming foods high in potassium can cause levels to build up in your blood.

High-Phosphorus Foods

Similar to potassium, kidneys also manage the balance of phosphorus in your body. High levels of phosphorus, often found in processed foods and sodas, can be harmful to kidneys, especially for those with kidney disease.

Artificial Sweeteners

Some studies suggest that consuming large amounts of artificial sweeteners may increase the risk of kidney function decline.

Carbonated Beverages

Drinks like soda are often high in phosphorus additives and sugars, which can put additional strain on the kidneys.

How Diet Can Slow CKD Progression

We have fairly established that diet and nutrition play a very big role in causing and worsening kidney damage, however, there's also truth in the saying "Your poison can also be your medicine".

A study on The Effect of Diet on the Survival of Patients with Chronic Kidney Disease *assessed the association between four lifestyle factors (diet, physical activity, body mass index—BMI, and smoking) with all-cause mortality among CKD participants. It demonstrated that individuals in the highest quartile of the weighted healthy lifestyle score had a 53% lower risk of death compared with those in the lowest quartile.*

You **NEED** to make changes to your diet when you have Chronic Kidney Disease.

The truth is, the renal diet is not easy to understand at first glance because it is NOT intuitive. Broccoli is a "YES", but Spinach "NOT TOO MUCH"... But they're both green vegetables? You have probably started searching for information on your own and found conflicting information on what foods you can eat and avoid.

These changes may include limiting your Sodium, Potassium, Protein, and Phosphorus (also known as your SPPP) to keep them below dangerous levels. So, what should you do?

Now, how come Renal Diet is not intuitive? It's because depending on your lab test results and your nutritionist's expert recommendation, you may need to restrict ALL of SPPP or only one of those nutrients. This would then change what food you can eat and what food you should avoid. This is why it's important to start by finding out what restriction applies to you.

With how much thought goes into it, you should also begin to think of your diet as part of your treatment.

What do we mean by thinking of diet as treatment?
Does that mean I shouldn't take medication from my MD?

CKD Chef Duane Sunwold shares...

"A colleague at Spokane Community College, my friend Erin, a Registered Dietitian, asked to see my labs and challenged to take me off animal protein for 90 days. It wasn't easy, but it was the best thing I could have ever done. Within two weeks, I started feeling better. Who knew, Kevin and Karl [referring to his kidneys] like plants, and they started doing their job again.

And in no time, I began to review my new kidney-friendly recipes healthy eating plan as the greatest culinary challenge a chef could have.

*As time went by, this new plant-based cuisine brought my creatinine level from 4.99 to a 0.8. Today, I'm in complete remission. **And I'm off all medication, with the blessing of my medical team, thanks to my diet.***

Taking control by making the necessary diet and lifestyle changes recommended by your medical team is part of self-management. But, don't forget that this is meant to COMPLEMENT your medical team's recommendations, not REPLACE them."

The Connection Between Diet and Dialysis

There is a long history linked between diet and dialysis and one study even divided these periods in history as different eras.

For a time, Potassium played a role in making or breaking the deal for a dialysis patient. The focus of this adjunct therapy to dialysis is the avoidance of high-potassium foods, putting lesser emphasis on giving plant-derived proteins that caused an imbalance in another nutrient's capacity to help in slowing disease progression.

Sodium has always been on the low as it's been earlier identified, to cause excessive thirst, thereby paving the way for increased fluid intake and overload.

Then, Phosphorus followed suit in the second era, where phosphate had been almost banned from a patient's diet and had been linked to a rising mortality rate.

When things weren't adding up, and dialysis had been failing, thanks to these extreme measures in nutrition, the biggest hurdle became malnutrition. Restricting almost all nutrients was by far the worst decision that has ever been made.

These scenarios should allow you to paint a better picture of the relationship between Diet and Chronic Kidney Disease where it's not just about limiting some and increasing some, but a well-thought-off treatment plan that revolves around your diet and nutrition.

Research on Diet and CKD

A review of more than 20 prospective cohort studies by A.C. van Westing et. al. of the Division of Human Nutrition and Health, Wageningen University focused on meat, fish, dairy, vegetables, fruit, coffee, tea, soft drinks, and dietary patterns, revealed convincing evidence that following a healthy dietary pattern increases the chances of lowering risks for Chronic Kidney Disease.

The study revealed benefits from plant-based food options and beverages e.g. coffee and some dairy. The components of unhealthy dieting that add stress to the kidneys were also identified to include red meats (especially processed ones) and sugar-sweetened beverages. Some other food groups included in the studies came back with inconclusive results, such as being neutral, but should not be automatically ruled out to be beneficial as there might be not enough evidence to conclude from.

The Importance of Controlling Blood Sugar and Blood Pressure

1. Control your blood pressure

I may have mentioned that your blood pressure is determined by **what you eat** and that you have to lower your SPPP intake to manage your blood pressure. For now, **the most important one is sodium.**

A huge portion of sodium in our diets comes from packaged and processed foods. And take note that your recommended daily sodium intake should be no less than 2,000 milligrams.

Aside from high blood pressure, a high sodium diet can result in other complication including:

- Swelling in the legs, and face.
- Heart failure
- Shortness of breath: Fluid can build up in the lungs which causes breathing problems.

Since **your target blood pressure should be lower than 130/80 mmHg,** lowering your sodium intake will improve your blood pressure. An additional reason to be good about sodium? Blood pressure medication becomes more effective when sodium levels are normal.

2. Manage your blood sugar levels

To prevent or slow down kidney damage, you have to keep your blood sugar controlled. It's usually done with diet, exercise, and taking insulin *(if needed)* or hypoglycemic pills *(helps lower your blood sugar level)*.

Being keen with the amount of sugar present in your food and beverages will really help make sure you don't damage your kidneys further and keep yourself at lower risk for developing diabetic kidney disease. Be deliberate in adjusting your sugar intake, may it be keeping yourself from adding more teaspoons of it in your coffee, indulging in that luscious devil's food cake, or even controlling your portions with that sweet juicy mango.

Renal Dieting may not be intuitive, but it doesn't mean it has to be impossible. Follow along in the next chapter as we explore the basics and the "what you can do" areas for CKD-Friendly Diet.

Chapter 2:
The Basics of a CKD-Friendly Diet

Scientific consensus underscores that dietary modifications can significantly affect Chronic Kidney Disease (CKD) progression. Optimal nutrition—emphasizing a low-protein, low-sodium, and high-fiber diet—has been shown to decelerate kidney function decline. Such dietary shifts not only support kidney health, but also mitigate associated risks like hypertension and diabetes. Therefore, bridging the knowledge gap in dietary management is critical for improving CKD outcomes.

What Makes a Diet CKD-Friendly?

As a general rule, anything that does not stress the kidneys, allowing them to function to their best, and making you feel great inside and out defines something as CKD-friendly. But that sure is too broad isn't it?

This question ultimately led me down the rabbit hole, as you may already know, conflicting information may be available just about everywhere, making this more complicated than it already is. But to make sure you don't go through the same, I have validated a working definition for a "CKD-Friendly Diet" through my personal experience with patients, and through digging deep into countless evidence-based studies over the years. Here it goes:

A CKD-Friendly diet should be one that slows down the progression of the disease to kidney failure. It should show clear signs of improving toxicity in the blood test results. It must help the patient maintain a favorable and sustainable nutritional status and should decrease the risk of any possible secondary complications.

The Role of Macronutrients and Micronutrients

Macronutrients are the nutrients we need in large amounts: proteins, carbohydrates, and fats. They're the main source of energy for our bodies. Let's take a closer look at how these macronutrients influence our health and our kidneys.

Proteins

Proteins are important for repairing and building tissues, but people with chronic kidney disease (CKD) should be careful about their intake. When our bodies use protein, they produce a waste product called urea. Healthy kidneys can remove this, but in CKD, it can build up in the blood and cause symptoms like fatigue and loss of appetite. Most guidelines suggest a low to moderate protein diet for CKD patients.

Carbohydrates

These provide our bodies with energy. People with CKD should focus on complex carbs (like whole grains and fruits) instead of simple ones (like sugar). However, those on dialysis may need extra carbs to balance the energy used during treatment.

Fats

Not all fats are bad. Healthy fats (like those in olive oil, avocados, and certain fish) may help reduce inflammation and improve heart health, which is particularly important for CKD patients.

Now let's also talk about micronutrients which includes vitamins and minerals. They are needed in smaller amounts, but they're still very important. Here are some of the micronutrients that are very relevant to Chronic Kidney Disease.

Sodium

In Chronic Kidney Disease (CKD), the kidneys struggle to balance sodium levels. Consuming too much sodium can cause fluid retention, leading to higher blood pressure and further kidney damage. It might also increase proteinuria, a key marker of CKD progression. Therefore, a diet low in sodium is often recommended for those with CKD to help manage blood pressure and prevent further deterioration of kidney function.

Potassium

Our bodies need potassium for nerve and muscle cell functioning, including for the heart. But in CKD, the kidneys may not be able to remove excess potassium, leading to high levels in the blood. This can be dangerous for the heart. Hence, potassium intake often needs to be limited.

Phosphorus

Phosphorus helps build strong bones and teeth, but in CKD, the kidneys can't excrete excess phosphorus, leading to high levels in the blood. This can cause bone and heart problems.

Vitamin D

It's important for bone health and the immune system. Yet, CKD often leads to vitamin D deficiency because the kidneys play a key role in activating vitamin D. Therefore, patients often need supplements.

Remember, every person is different, and dietary needs can vary greatly among people with CKD. It's crucial to work closely with your healthcare team to create a diet plan that's right for you.

Importance of Individual Dietary Requirements

From the beginning, I cannot emphasize enough the fact that CKD care and the management of it is not generic, and that every patient's general wellbeing should be the top basis of their individualized care.

The same is true with renal diet, as we have established that it is part of your treatment plan. Now you may ask, "what is the importance of individual's dietary requirements?" That's a great question! Individual dietary requirements are important because they take into account a person's unique needs and circumstances. Here's why this matters, especially for people with chronic kidney disease (CKD).

1. Stage of CKD

Different stages of CKD require different dietary adjustments. For example, in early stages, you may only need to watch your protein intake, but in later stages, you might need to limit nutrients like potassium and phosphorus too.

2. Other Health Conditions

Many people with CKD also have other health conditions like diabetes or heart disease. These conditions often require different or additional dietary modifications.

3. Nutritional Status

People with CKD are at risk of malnutrition. They need a diet that ensures they get enough calories and nutrients to stay healthy, but doesn't overload their kidneys. This balance can be tricky and depends on factors like age, sex, weight, and physical activity level.

4. Personal Preferences and Lifestyle

A person's cultural background, personal tastes, and lifestyle also play a big role. A diet that doesn't consider these factors may be hard to stick to and could lower the quality of life.

5. Treatment Plan

People on dialysis have different dietary needs than those who aren't. For example, dialysis patients often need more protein to compensate for losses during treatment.

Because of all these factors, it's crucial to work with a dietitian or healthcare provider to create a personalized eating plan. This plan should meet your nutritional needs, be realistic for your lifestyle, and accommodate your personal preferences.

Remember, managing CKD isn't just about avoiding certain foods. It's about creating a healthy, enjoyable diet that supports your overall well-being. And that's best achieved when the diet is tailored to you!

The Role of Different Food Groups

Proteins: Animal vs. Plant-Based

Does switching to a plant-based diet help?

Protein could be tricky for Chronic Kidney Disease patients. While it may be one of the essential nutrients for a healthy, normal kidney, too much protein is bad for a malfunctioning one. A plant-based diet is **beneficial if you have early kidney disease.** Plant-based foods have fewer calories compared to their animal-based counterpart and are beneficial if you have early kidney disease.

A plant-based diet helps lower blood pressure and cholesterol thereby reducing heart-related diseases. It also improves antioxidant levels that fight against cell damage. Minimizing animal-based food lowers acid buildup in the blood, which puts less stress on the kidneys.

It is recommended to eat just small portions of protein foods that may be sourced from animals, e.g. chicken, fish, meat, eggs, and dairy, and from plants, e.g. beans, nuts, and grains.

Recommended sources of proteins for CKD patients include fish, chicken breast, low-fat soy products, and low-fat dairy products.

Be sure to talk to your dietitian to get the specific amount of protein that your body—especially your kidney—needs.

Animal-protein foods

- Meat, such as pork, beef, chicken, turkey, duck
- Eggs
- Dairy products, such as milk, yogurt, cheese
- Fish

Plant-protein foods

High protein

- Beans, peas, lentils
- Soy foods, such as soy milk, tofu

- Nuts and nut spreads, such as almond butter, peanut butter, soy nut butter
- Sunflower seeds

Low protein

- Bread, tortillas
- Oatmeal, grits, cereals
- Pasta, noodles, rice
- Rice milk (not enriched)

TINY HABIT 1. After I know my recommended protein intake, I will integrate a plant-based substitute to my kidney diet.

But what if I'm not ready to make that switch yet?

If you don't like to prepare or cook them at all, CKD Chef Duane suggested that you can fill half your plate with fruits and vegetables. Quarter the other half into starch, rice, and pasta. While the other quarter is protein.

And when you go grocery shopping, you go through and look at the meat section and pick your meal. CKD Chef Duane thinks it's such a creative way to live when he went through the produce section.

But more importantly, you need to plan your meals ahead of time. In your meal planning, you can implement things like beans, lentils, portobello mushroom, or tofu as a great protein source of your diet.

Yes, I know that most people probably don't like the texture or the taste of tofu. BUT you can get creative with some great tasting tofu recipes.

Here's another, you can take cashew nuts, soak them in hot water, and then drain them. Once you're done, you can puree them in your tofu in a food processor, which results in a thick texture. And yes, you can season it anyway you like. You can do a southwest flavor or you can use italian herbs and make them into a stuffing like zucchini boats or pasta shells.

And if you're having trouble figuring out what recipes you would like to prepare, Northwest Kidney Center has shared some of its recipes to help you.

As for timing like that souffle, plan ahead; **people who plan ahead almost always make a healthier choice than those we make because we don't have enough time.**

The Right Kind of Carbohydrates

Now, time to talk about the other nutrient factors to consider: **fat and sugar** *(carbohydrates).*

Earlier in this chapter, we touched the basics of macronutrients or the three (3) major nutrients found in foods: Protein, carbohydrates, and fat. Carbohydrates are a **major fuel source for your body.**

When you eat carbohydrates, your body turns them into glucose *(the energy source for the cells in the body).* With insulin, cells are able to use that energy to perform everyday functions and help you feel your best. Besides providing energy for your body, foods that are rich in carbohydrates are good sources of vitamins, minerals, fiber, and other compounds that help protect your body. Some carbohydrate foods actually contain fiber. Fiber plays an important role in protecting your heart, blood vessels, and colon.

As I may have previously mentioned a couple of times, once you are diagnosed with Chronic Kidney Disease, you are at risk of having health complications like heart disease, which is the leading cause of death, especially in dialysis patients.

So, high fiber diets will help lower your cholesterol levels and reduce your risk for heart attack and other cardiovascular conditions. You need to ask your dietitian which high fiber foods may work in your kidney diet. But for now, I want to share with you how CKD Chef Duane did it.

Since CKD Chef Duane finds sugar addictive, the more he uses it, the more he craves it, he stopped himself from that cycle by slowly weaning himself down. **He uses and eats fresh fruits as much as possible for dessert.** A trick he learned from a clever chef in Scottsdale is that he would make smaller protein portions and give the customers larger portions of fresh fruit for dessert.

"The flavors eaten during the last course are the ones that stay on our palates the longest", he said. So, when he applied what he learned, he didn't feel deprived of the foods that he likes.

The Importance of Healthy Fats

Let's move on to fat...

For fat, it also provides energy and helps produce hormones that regulate blood pressure and other heart functions and carries fat-soluble vitamins. But it's also important to know about fat sources because eating the wrong kinds and too much of **it increases the risk of clogged vessels and heart problems.**

You should talk to a dietitian about healthy and unhealthy sources of fat since for example, there are saturated fats and trans-fatty acids like red meat, poultry, whole milk, and butter could raise blood cholesterol levels and clog blood vessels. He or she can suggest healthy ways to include fat in the diet especially if your diet needs more calories. Vegetable oils such as corn or safflower oil are healthier than animal fats such as butter or lard.

But then again, you **should speak to your dietitian** before moving forward. However, CKD Chef Duane took as much fat from recipes as he could without giving up his goal of keeping the flavor in.

How? He uses vegetable stock in place of salad oils when making salad dressings. Another gifted chef instructor at his culinary school taught him that technique.

Fluids and CKD - Hydration and Fluid Restrictions

Hydration is important for everyone, but it can be a delicate balance for people with chronic kidney disease (CKD). Here's why:

The kidneys' job is to filter waste products from the blood and regulate fluids in the body. When they're not working well, they can't remove excess fluid. This excess fluid can build up in the body, a condition called fluid overload, which can cause problems like:

- High blood pressure, where extra fluid increases the volume of blood in your veins and arteries, raising your blood pressure.
- Swelling. You might notice it in your legs, ankles, or hands. This is called edema.

- Shortness of breath. Again, fluid can accumulate in the lungs, making it hard to breathe.

Because of these risks, people with advanced CKD or those on dialysis often need to limit their fluid intake. However, the amount of fluid restriction can vary significantly from person to person. It depends on factors like the stage of CKD, urine output, whether the person is on dialysis and the type of dialysis they're receiving.

On the other hand, it's also important to avoid dehydration, which can happen if you don't drink enough water. Dehydration can cause headaches, and dizziness, and in severe cases, can further damage the kidneys.

Remember, "fluid" doesn't just refer to water. It includes anything that turns into liquid at room temperature, like ice cream, gelatin, and soup, as well as beverages like coffee, tea, and soda. And because managing fluid intake can be complex in CKD, it's essential to work closely with your healthcare team who can help you figure out the right balance for your unique situation.

Choosing the Right Beverages

Certainly, choosing the right kind of beverage when you have CKD involves a few considerations. Here are some tips to guide you:

1. **Avoid high-potassium drinks.** Some beverages, like orange juice and tomato juice, are high in potassium, which can be dangerous in CKD. A safer choice might be apple juice or cranberry juice, which are lower in potassium.

2. **Limit high-phosphorus drinks.** Dark-colored sodas often contain phosphorus additives, which can be harmful for people with CKD. Instead, choose light-colored or clear sodas, like lemon-lime soda or ginger ale.

3. **Watch out for caffeine and alcohol**. Both can dehydrate you, so it's important to consume them in moderation. Water, herbal tea, or decaffeinated coffee can be good alternatives.

4. **Stay away from high-sodium drinks.** Some vegetable juices and canned soups can be high in sodium. Look for low-sodium versions or make your own at home.

5. **Be mindful of fluids in foods.** Remember, foods that are liquid at room temperature, like ice cream and gelatin, count towards your fluid intake.

6. **Water is always a good choice.** But remember to keep track of how much you drink, especially if you've been advised to limit your fluid intake.

Remember, these are general guidelines. The best beverage for you will depend on your individual circumstances, including your stage of CKD, any other health conditions, and your personal preferences. Always check with your healthcare team or dietitian to make sure your choices fit within your dietary plan.

Having learned of the "basics", the science, and the important foundational truths about the CKD diet, I would like to take you more into what it means to apply it to your lifestyle. I will be teaching more "TINY HABITS" that you can do in order to start incorporating changes into your diet and really get into that journey of making that positive change toward health.

Chapter 3:

The Role of Protein, Potassium, Phosphorus, and Sodium in CKD

Understanding the impact of these nutrients on chronic kidney disease (CKD) progression can be quite surprising. Here's a fact about each nutrient and its relationship to CKD:

Sodium

A study found that people with CKD who consumed high-sodium diets had twice the risk of progressing to end stage renal disease. This shows how a high-sodium diet can accelerate the progression of CKD.

Protein

Research suggests that a low-protein diet can slow the progression of CKD and reduce the symptoms. In one study, a low-protein diet reduced the risk of kidney failure by 32%.

Potassium

While it is important to avoid high potassium levels (hyperkalemia) in CKD, it's also crucial not to have too low levels (hypokalemia). A study found that both hyperkalemia and hypokalemia are associated with an increased risk of death in people with CKD.

Phosphorus

High phosphorus levels can lead to serious health problems, including heart disease, bone disease, and even death. Surprisingly, even within the "normal" range, higher phosphorus levels can be harmful. A study found a 27% higher risk of death in CKD patients with phosphorus levels at the high end of the normal range, compared to those at the low end.

These statistics underline how important it is to manage these nutrients in your diet when you have CKD. As always, the best way to do this is by working closely with your healthcare team.

Protein and CKD

Let's start by making one thing clear: **protein is good for you.**

Without protein, your body won't function the way it's supposed to. It's needed for most bodily processes, especially for growth, maintenance, and repair. It also plays a major role in building up muscle and fighting infection.

But here's the catch— Whenever your body breaks down protein from food, a waste product called urea is produced. High levels of urea can cause fatigue and poor appetite. Too much protein in the body can also cause a buildup of creatinine, another by-product of metabolism as protein is used up. Creatinine, whether you're aware or not, is one of the key determinants of kidney damage.

Your kidneys work to remove these by-products from your system. That means, *the more protein you eat, the more work your kidneys have to do.* And that's basically the reason why **a low-protein diet** may be recommended by your nutritionist. Give your kidneys a lighter workload. This will help you slow down your kidney's deterioration, if not maintain the level of kidney function you still have.

Now that you understand why it's important to control your protein intake, let's explore the **how.**

We were able to discuss the importance of protein and the negative effects it can have on your kidneys, but this chapter will focus on the causes of too much protein in the urine *(proteinuria)*, what lab tests should be done, and what the next step is.

Protein is needed for most bodily processes, especially for growth, maintenance, and repair. It also plays a major role in building up muscle and fighting infection. Without protein, your body won't function the way it's supposed to. When healthy kidneys filter fluid, minerals, and wastes from the blood, they usually do not allow large amounts of serum protein to escape into the urine.

But when the kidneys are not filtering properly, protein in urine *(proteinuria)* **can occur**. For this reason, an abnormal amount of protein is then present in the urine. Having too much protein in the urine is not good for the kidneys because it's a sign of kidneys damage AND can scar the kidney because your kidneys are not able to remove all the extra waste. In most cases, proteinuria has no symptoms but if kidney damage gets worse and large amounts of protein escape from your blood through your urine, you may notice the following symptoms:

- Foamy or bubbly pee
- Swelling (edema) in your hands, feet, belly, and face
- Peeing more often
- Shortness of breath

41

- Fatigue
- Loss of appetite
- Upset stomach and vomiting
- Muscle cramps at night

What causes proteinuria?

There are actually a few causes to proteinuria, so be sure to take note of your other symptoms that will help your doctor **identify the underlying cause**:

1 **Dehydration** - This happens when your body loses too much fluid. Your body uses water to deliver nutrients, like proteins to the kidneys but without enough fluid, it will have difficulty doing so. In turn, the kidneys can't properly recapture proteins. It ends up in the urine instead.

2 **High Blood Pressure** - High blood pressure *(hypertension)* can weaken the blood vessels in the kidneys. This decreases their ability to reabsorb to protein, which flows into the urine.

3 **Diabetes** - With diabetes, high blood sugar forces the kidneys to over filter the blood. This can cause kidney damage, allowing protein to leak into the urine.

4 **Glomerulonephritis** - When glomeruli filter blood, they reabsorb protein. But if they're injured, protein can pass through and enter the urine.

5 **Chronic Kidney Disease** - CKD may cause proteinuria in the early stages, but it usually doesn't cause any noticeable symptoms.

6 **Autoimmune Diseases** - The immune system normally produces antibodies and immunoglobulins that fight foreign organisms. But if you have an autoimmune disease, the

immune system makes antibodies and immunoglobulins that attack the body's tissues. These substances are called autoantibodies.

If the autoantibodies injure the glomeruli, inflammation can occur. This leads to kidney damage, and eventually, proteinuria.

What lab tests should be done?

The only way to diagnose proteinuria is through a **urine test,** which measures the amount of protein in your urine. The urine test takes place in a doctor's office. During the procedure, you have to urinate into a specimen cup which the doctor places a dipstick, or a small plastic stick coated with chemicals, into the urine sample.

If your urine has too much protein, **it changes color.** The rest of the urine will be sent to a lab where it will be examined under a microscope. A doctor might also use the following tests to determine what's causing your proteinuria:

- **24-hour urine collection.** In a 24-hour urine test, your urine is collected over 24 hours and sent to a lab.
- **Glomerular Filtration Rate blood test.** This test checks your kidney function.
- **Imaging tests.** You may get an ultrasound or CT Scan, which takes detailed photos of your kidneys and urinary tract.
- **Kidney biopsy.** A sample of your kidney is removed and examined for signs of kidney damage.

Can proteinuria be treated?

So treatment depends on figuring out what caused it. You might not need treatment if proteinuria is mild or lasts only a short time. But it's crucial to treat kidney disease before it leads to kidney failure. Your doctor might prescribe medication, especially if you have diabetes and/or high blood pressure. Most people will take one of two types of blood pressure medicine:

- ACE Inhibitors (angiotensin-converting enzyme inhibitors)
- ARBs (angiotensin receptor blockers)

What should I do next?

If you have temporary or mild proteinuria, you likely won't need treatment. But if you have consistent proteinuria, you'll need to treat the underlying condition. Treatment may include:

- Dietary changes
- Weight loss
- Blood pressure medication
- Diabetes medication
- Dialysis

Protein could be tricky for CKD Patients like yourself. While it may be one of the essential nutrients for a healthy, normal kidney, too much protein is bad for a malfunctioning one.

Take note that all foods contain protein, but there are two general types of sources you can choose from:

- **High-value proteins refers to protein you get from animal sources.**

  These are easier for your body to use, but can also be rich in fat and cholesterol. **They are often also high in phosphorus, so you might have to limit your intake of them.**

- **Low-value proteins refers to protein you get from plant sources**. Vegetables, cereals, beans, bread, rice, and pasta or noodles are some good examples.

To maintain a healthy diet, it's important to strike a good balance between these two.

Since they're usually high in fat, high-value protein should only make up around 70% of your total protein intake. The rest (30%) should come from low-value proteins—so don't forget your grains and vegetables!

TINY HABIT 2: After I pick a high-value protein, I will add a low-value protein to my shopping cart.

Most processed foods are meat. Animal protein produces **high amounts of acid in the blood that can be harmful to the kidneys** and cause acidosis. Acidosis is an illness where malfunctioning kidneys cannot eliminate acid from the body fast enough. Although protein may be needed for growth and repair, your kidney-friendly diet should be supplemented with fruits and vegetables.

Renal dietitians recommend that instead of animal protein from ground beef, shrimp, salmon, tuna, chicken breast, roasted chicken, or their processed versions, plant-based protein (from beans, nuts, or whole grains) or these lower-protein alternatives are preferable:

- Chili con carne
- Beef stew
- Egg substitutes
- Tofu
- Imitation crab meat

TINY HABIT 3: After I decide on a lower-protein alternative, I will apply one of the handy tips listed below.

Controlling your portions is a very handy technique in keeping your protein intake within your limits. Here are some handy tips to get you started:

FOR SANDWICHES:

- Slice your meat very thinly. This way, the flavor is spread out and the portions look larger.

- Cut your bread more thickly. This will help you feel fuller even with less meat.

- Try breads with a more distinct taste, like rye or sourdough, to add more flavor.

- Fill up your sandwich with other ingredients, like lettuce, cucumbers, parsley, alfalfa sprouts, water chestnuts, celery, or even apples, instead of protein sources.

FOR SOUPS:

- Use low protein milk substitutes when cooking cream soups. Or stay away from them altogether.

- Add relatively low protein ingredients like pasta or rice to make your soup more hearty and filling.

FOR MAIN DISHES:

- Have grains and vegetables as the main dish more often, and use high-value proteins like meat as side dishes.

- Eat more kebabs. Add more fruits and vegetables and use smaller pieces of meat.

- Adjust your casserole recipes. Use smaller amounts of protein than the recipe calls for, and increase the starch (pasta or rice) to make up for it.
- Mix protein with rice and pasta often. Pasta with ground meat and fried rice recipes are good examples.
- Chef salads are great for you. Just toss lettuce and fresh veggies with small strips of egg and meat, and you've got a quick and tasty meal.
- Use cheeses with stronger tastes, like Parmesan or Romano. That way, you'll only need a small amount to get a good flavor.
- Increase your servings of pasta, rice, and bread. Cutting down protein from your diet can cause you to eat less calories than usual. Make up for the difference by eating more of these relatively low protein foods.

I know that at this point in the book, it seems like a lot to take in but don't forget that taking this step is important to achieving your kidney health goal.

*"You don't have to see the whole staircase. Just take the **first step**."*

- Martin Luther King Jr.

Potassium's Impact on CKD

Potassium is a fairly common nutrient which can be found in almost any food. It is responsible for **keeping your nerves and muscles healthy** and **maintaining the normal rhythm of your heart beat.** The kidneys help maintain your potassium at normal level. However, if your potassium levels are too high or too low, **it is not good.**

So, *what happens if my potassium levels are too high or too low?*

When the kidneys can no longer remove excess potassium, it only builds up in the body which causes it to rise. Having too much potassium affects the way your heart and muscles work. Therefore, **your heart may beat irregularly**, which in worst cases, **can cause a heart attack.** And if your potassium level is too low *(also known as **hyperkalemia**),* it can cause **weakness, numbness, and may develop abnormal heart rhythms.**

To avoid these complications, it is important that you **HAVE TO** consult your kidney doctor and nutritionist and work on a plan that will help keep your potassium level in normal range based on what your lab results show.

So, what is the secret to maintaining potassium levels?

The answer: MODERATION.

According to The National Kidney Foundation, the normal amount in a typical healthy American is **3,500 to 4,500 milligrams per day.** For patients with a potassium-restricted diet, they can go as low as **2,000 mg per day.** However, it depends on what your physician or dietitian advises you to take based on your health.

You'll need a blood test to confirm whether your current potassium levels are high or not and you can use these values as a general reference:

Blood Potassium Level (mmol/L)	Description
3.5 – 5.0	your blood potassium level is **normal**
5.1 – 6.0	your blood potassium level is **elevated**
6.0 and above	your blood potassium level is **exceedingly high**

TINY HABIT 4: After I decide on a vegetable/fruit to add to my shopping list, I'll ask my doctor or dietician if it is good for my potassium level

You have to be careful with what you eat, as well as how much, is the most important point in a low-potassium diet. In general, any food that contains more than 200 mg potassium per serving is **high in potassium.** So, you'll have to start watching out for high-potassium foods such as bananas, potatoes, spinach, brussels sprouts, and avocados.

TINY HABIT 5: After I get home from shopping, I will try leaching one of my vegetables

Leaching is a process that helps reduce the potassium content of food. It means that you don't have to give up high potassium vegetables, you just need more time to prepare them. Here's how you can do it:

For beets, carrots, potatoes, sweet potatoes, rutabagas, and winter squash:

1. Peel and place vegetables in cold water (to avoid darkening)
2. Slice into 1/8 inch thick pieces
3. Briefly rinse in warm water
4. Soak in warm water for a minimum of 2 hours. Use ten times the amount of water to the amount of vegetables. For example, 10 cups of water for 1 cup of vegetables.
5. Rinse in warm water again for a few seconds
6. Cook vegetables. Use 5 times the amount of water to the amount of vegetables. For example, 5 cups of water for 1 cup of vegetables.

Now remember, although leaching is an effective process, it only **reduces potassium but DOES NOT eliminate it entirely**.

Potassium and phosphorus may be listed on a label in milligrams or percent daily value (% DV), but they are not required to be on a label. If potassium and phosphorus are not listed, it does not mean that they are not present in that food. Your needs are different from the daily value when you have CKD. If percent daily values for potassium and phosphorus are listed, you can use them to help with your diet.

Ask your dietitian about your potassium needs. Some foods with

	Low Potassium	Medium	High	Very high
mg per serving	<100	101-200	201-300	>300
% DV	<3	3-6	6-9	over 9

of not tify ted

from highest to lowest quantity on a food label.

As mentioned, Potassium does not need to be declared on a food label. If it is not listed, it does NOT mean there is no potassium in your food. Your needs are different from the daily value of a person without CKD.

Aside from cooking foods that are low in potassium, you may need to completely stopped drinking fruit and vegetable juice since they can be a high source of digestible potassium. I strongly recommend that you to get a list of high and low potassium foods from your kidney doctor or dietitian.

Now, you won't be able to understand all of these in the first try, but with practice, it will become part of your routine.

Sodium and CKD

In the right amounts, sodium is actually an important part of one's diet. Our bodies need this mineral in order to:

- Keep our muscles and nerves functioning,
- Keep our cells properly hydrated, and;
- Maintain our blood volume and blood pressure, among others.

Unfortunately, since most foods naturally have some sodium in them + we love table salt, it is common for people to go overboard and have too much.

In fact, the National Kidney Foundation (NKF) estimates that on average, **Americans consume 50% more sodium than the recommended daily amount.**

Normally, the kidneys are responsible for removing excess sodium. But when they aren't functioning at full capacity, a buildup is inevitable. This can cause a lot of problems, such as:

- Puffiness and swelling, mostly in the legs and ankles,
- Fluid retention around the heart and lungs,
- Shortness of breath,
- High blood pressure, and;
- Decreased kidney function, due to damaged blood vessels in the kidneys.

To avoid these complications, the USDA advises those with kidney conditions to limit themselves to **1500 mg of sodium per day,** in accordance with the USDA's Dietary Guidelines for Americans 2010.

So, *what are TINY habits you can do NOW to control your sodium intake?*

TINY HABIT 6: After I pick something from the grocery shelf, I will compare it with 2 other brands to choose the one with the lowest sodium

Reading food labels is a step in the right direction. Look at the *Nutrition Facts* section of the food item you bought and see how much **sodium** is in it. You can use this screenshot as a guide:

% Daily Value	Amount of sodium per serving	What it means...
Less than 5%	Less than **125 mg**	**Good choice** – a low sodium product that you can have often
5 – 10%	Less than **250 mg**	**Good choice** – a low sodium product that fits your low sodium diet easily
10 – 20%	Between **250 – 500 mg**	**Be cautious** – this can still fit into a low sodium diet, but you'll have to observe caution
More than 20%	More than **500 mg**	**Beware** – this is a high sodium product that should not be eaten in a low sodium diet

*Adapted from information by The Kidney Foundation of Canada

What you can do next time, is make a simple swap. For example, if you decide to buy chicken stock…

…pick up the brand you usually get and look at the sodium per 100g

...pick up a 2nd brand and look at the sodium per 100g

...pick up a 3rd brand and look at the sodium per 100g

...choose the one with the **lowest sodium per 100g**

Do this for **one** grocery item every time you shop. Don't try to replace everything in one go, we're creating easy, tiny habits that you can do every time!

TINY HABIT 7: After I go through my shopping list, I will add one fresh ingredient to my shopping cart

According to data from the Centers for Disease Control and Prevention (CDC), **more than 75% of the sodium Americans consume comes from processed food, pre-packaged meals, and restaurant food.** So, a significant way to cut down on your sodium intake is to choose fresh ingredients when cooking.

TINY HABIT 8: After I pass by the salt aisle, I will get an additional non-salt spice to try

One more surefire way of reducing your sodium intake is to switch up your cooking methods. **Instead of using salt on your recipes, use other herbs and spices to add flavor to your dishes.** Some very good examples of these are the following:

Spice	Food its Best Paired With
Allspice	beef, eggs, fish, fruits, vegetables, beverages, baked products, desserts
Basil	lamb, fish, eggs, vegetables, sauces
Bay Leaf	beef, chicken, veal, fish
Cinnamon	chicken, pork, fruits, baked products, beverages, vegetables

Cloves	beef, pork, fruits
Curry (salt-free)	beef, chicken, lamb, veal, eggs
Dill	chicken, veal, fish, vegetables
Ginger	chicken, pork, fruits, vegetables, baked products, beverages
Marjoram	eggs, fish, meat, poultry
Mustard Powder	meat, poultry, fish, eggs, vegetables
Parsley	beef, chicken, fish, salads, sauces
Rosemary	beef, lamb, chicken, turkey
Sage	meat, fish, stuffing, vegetables
Savory	egg dishes, meat, poultry, stuffing, rice, vegetables
Tarragon	chicken, fish, meat, egg dishes, sauces, vegetables
Thyme	fish, meat, poultry, eggs, stuffing, vegetables

Phosphorus and Your Kidneys

Fact: Every nutrient we take into our body does serve a purpose.

For example, sodium helps the body regulate its fluids. Protein, on the other hand, mainly builds our muscles, tissues, and organs. And potassium adds to the functions of the two, helping muscle-building and fluid regulation.

For phosphorus, it is important for your bones and joints. It works with Calcium and Vitamin D in your body to keep your bones healthy and strong. When you have healthy kidneys, they help keep the right amount of phosphorus in the body. But with Chronic Kidney Disease, your kidneys cannot do that job as well as before, allowing phosphorus to build up to dangerous levels in the blood. Too much phosphorus may cause bones to lose calcium instead, making them brittle and weak. This lost calcium can pile up in blood vessels, causing them to harden, leading to even more problems down the line—**joint pain, itchy skin, and lung, eye, or heart problems**, to name a few.

Excess phosphorus in the body is usually filtered out by the kidneys and excreted. But when kidney function is compromised, it can be difficult to keep blood phosphorus levels within the healthy range.

The normal blood phosphorus level is 2.5–4.5 mg/dL (milligrams per deciliter), and your kidneys are largely responsible for maintaining that normal range. Any excess phosphorus is excreted through urine.

To avoid those health concerns, you need to keep your blood phosphorus level within the normal range. This is why as much as possible, you **should avoid processed foods**. Additionally, this will also help you limit your sodium, because that's also high in processed foods.

So what steps can I do to help limit phosphorus intake?

1. Check food labels for "phos-" ingredients.

Yes, the Nutrition Facts section of food labels don't indicate how much phosphorus is in a particular food item. But, they do indicate their phosphorus additives in their list of ingredients. All you have to do is steer clear of foods with "phos-" additives in them. Components like:

- Calcium **phos**phate
- Dicalcium **phos**phate
- Disodium **phos**phate
- Monopotassium **phos**phate
- Monosodium **phos**phate
- **Phos**phoric acid
- Pyrophosphate poly**phos**phate
- Sodium hexameta-**phos**phate
- Tetrasodium pyro**phos**phate
- Tricalcium **phos**phate
- Trisodium **phos**phate

Always remember to be extra vigilant when grocery shopping!

TINY HABIT 9. After I pick a canned ingredient, I will check food labels for "phos-" ingredients.

2. Talk to your health professional about phosphate binders.

I'm always hesitant about recommending medication. People tend to become overly dependent on drugs, and they neglect what diet and lifestyle changes can do. But if your phosphorus level is getting out of hand, then you can talk to your healthcare professionals about using **phosphate binders.**

Phosphate (or phosphorus) binders are medications that help you control phosphorus levels in your body. They absorb excess phosphorus from the food you eat and help you pass it out of your body through your stool. There are many types of this -- pills, powders, liquids, and even chewable tablets.

HOWEVER... Keep this in mind: **DO NOT take phosphate binders without the approval of a doctor or dietitian.** The assessment of a medical professional is absolutely necessary before starting this type of medication.

3. Switch to a low-phosphorus diet.

As suggested by the National Kidney Foundation (NKF), **the ideal phosphorus intake limit for people with kidney conditions is 800-1000 mg daily.** But limiting this nutrient is easier said than done. You see, most of the things that we enjoy are actually high-phosphorus food items, such as:

- Organ meat
- Dairy products
- Beans
- Lentils
- Nuts
- Cola
- Bran cereals
- Oatmeal

But you don't need to worry much about it, as there are low-phosphorus alternatives, such as these:

- Fresh fruits and vegetables

- Breads
- Pasta
- Rice
- Milk
- Corn and rice cereals
- Light color soda

TINY HABIT 10. After checking food labels for "phos-" ingredients, I will pick a low-phosphorus alternative.

I hope that this chapter has fully equipped you with the right knowledge that you need to move forward not only with this book but towards your journey to better kidney health. Flip through the next chapter and we will put what you have learned here into practical and actionable applications.

I would love to hear from you!

It's through your support and reviews that my book is able to reach other Chronic Kidney Disease patients who are still struggling to figure out how they could take a proactive approach in managing their CKD. Please take 60 seconds to kindly leave a review on Amazon. Please scan the QR code below, alternatively, you may use the link provided in your Amazon order.

Please follow these simple steps to rate/review my book:

1. Open the camera on your phone

2. Hover it over the QR code below

3. You may also type this link on your phone or browser: **https://go.renaltracker.com/bookreview**

4. Rate/Review my book

I appreciate you taking the time, your review will surely make a difference.

Thank you!

Janeth Kingston

Chapter 4:
Translating Diet into Daily Meals

"**H**ow can meal planning and portion control strategies be effectively integrated into the daily routine of a patient with CKD to manage their protein, potassium, phosphorus, and sodium intake, while also maintaining a balanced and enjoyable diet?"

Importance of Meal Planning

A kidney-friendly meal plan is essential for people with Chronic Kidney Disease. The nutritional needs of people with CKD differ and change as their disease progresses. Which is why it's important to talk to a registered dietitian to find a kidney-friendly meal plan that works best for you since following a healthy diet plan can also possibly slow down CKD progression.

The National Kidney Foundation defines a well-balanced diet as a meal plan that "gives you the right amounts of protein, calories, vitamins, and minerals each day. Eating a healthy diet, staying physically active, and taking all your medicines as prescribed are all important parts to keeping you healthy and feeling well." To know which nutrient to personally restrict and the right amounts you will need, you have to ask your renal dietitian (who would consult closely with your nephrologist).

CKD Chef Duane, as you have already known, gave a talk at the American Society of Nephrology Kidney Week, the world-leading congress on kidney science, and said this:

"Because I have kidneys on crutches, I got to explore a whole new world of cooking. Creating kidney-friendly diets is one of the most interesting culinary challenges I have ever had to face in my professional cooking career."

CKD Chef Duane agreed that salt is the most boring flavor there is. Salt masks taste. Unfortunately, humans are programmed to crave salt. It was scarce for our ancestors. However, once you learn to cook with less salt, you will find that you will start to hate salt. Importantly, when you start replacing salt, you will discover a whole new range of tasty food that is healthier for your kidneys too!

Sticking to a healthy diet plan can be challenging. However, you can see this as an opportunity to feel and eat better, have a greater quality of life and do more of what you enjoy.

What can you do?

Here are 5 actionable ways to Kickstarting Kidney-friendly meal plan:

Kickstarting Kidney-friendly Meals 1: <u>Consult a Registered Dietitian</u>

According to an article in the Journal of the Academy of Nutrition and Dietetics, 90 percent of non-dialysis kidney disease patients never meet with a dietitian. The authors added that adults with CKD are poorly informed on how diet influences disease management and progression.

Working with a registered dietitian is crucial in managing your CKD. Your dietitian will track your nutritional health and recommend customized meal plans and food substitutes that are nutritious as they are enjoyable. Dietitians will also check your blood results to suggest adjustments to balance your nutrition.

Kickstarting Kidney-friendly Meals 2: <u>Think forward</u>

Tweaking your lifestyle is necessary for healthy kidneys. However, you don't have to make such drastic changes immediately otherwise, you'd fall short on your goals. A very concrete and useful way to bring about the change you want is learning to plan. Take small, important steps towards making these changes. Consider the following:

- Food has natural sodium in them. Try to limit your sodium intake from 3 teaspoons to 1 or limit sodium intake at 20% to 40% to avoid making your food taste bland. You may not even notice the reduced sodium content.
- Plan out your daily or weekly meals.
- Write down a shopping list and follow it (this will save you a great deal of money, too).
- Design how you will prepare the food and what to put in it.
- Decide on where you will eat—home, restaurant, at the picnic with loved ones, or someone else's home, etc.

TRIVIA:

A 2017 study among French adults published in the International Journal of Behavioral Nutrition and Physical Activity revealed that meal planning encouraged home meal preparation which is linked to improved diet quality.

It will seem usual and effortless to keep up with your new diet once you get into the practice of planning meals. A small venture of time and effort, they say, brings a great return.

Kickstarting Kidney-friendly Meals 3: <u>Keep a food journal</u>

Keeping a nutrition journal will help you keep track of how you feel, based on what you eat, how much you weigh, what questions you have, and what you will learn. You can use it to write down:

- Daily or weekly food and beverage intake. Include portion sizes and how the foods are prepared.
- Your notes about exercise, meal plans, what you've learned from your research, readings, and experience on CKD and nutrition, etc.
- Stuff you want to mention to your doctor and/or dietitian, e.g. food choices and preference, preparation, etc.

The US Department of Health and Human Services-National Institute of Diabetes and Digestive and Kidney Diseases gives an informative guideline on the intake of the crucial nutrients such as calories, protein, fat, sodium, potassium, and phosphorus.

With good nutrition—eating the right foods and drinking the right beverages— a CKD patient may avoid or postpone some health problems since nutritional needs can vary as CKD progresses

Kickstarting Kidney-friendly Meals 4: <u>Learn to read nutrition labels</u>

Food labels are helpful in understanding the nutrients that food has. It guides you in choosing the right food for your CKD. Food labels have percent daily values based on the Food and Drug Administration (FDA) recommended a 2000 calorie diet.

Consult with your dietitian to learn reading nutrition labels as well as your diet restrictions.

Kickstarting Kidney-friendly Meals 5: Eyes on the Prize: Stay healthy!

The National Kidney Foundation lists down reasons good nutrition is important for people with CKD:

- It provides energy for daily tasks
- It prevents infection
- It helps you avoid muscle-mass loss
- It helps maintain a healthy weight
- It slows down the progression of the kidney disease

TRIVIA:

A 2018 study by researchers from the Harvard T.H. Chan School of Public Health showed that there are five areas of healthy living worth focusing on: healthy diet, healthy physical activity level, healthy body weight, smoking, and moderate alcohol intake.

Just one healthy habit (and it didn't matter which one) … just one… extended life expectancy by two years in men and women. It goes on to point out that "Not surprisingly, the more healthy habits people had, the longer their lifespan."

Embracing a CKD diet plan doesn't mean self-deprivation. You don't have to entirely give up the flavor as well as your favorite food to stick to a healthier lifestyle. Talk to your registered dietitian to find healthy alternatives to your favorite food. Having great support and the right perspective can help you stick to a healthy CKD meal plan.

Meal Planning Tips for Success

Let's get to the benefits of a specific kind of self-monitoring: food logging or the practice of writing down what you ate so you can get feedback on it.

The reason why you should monitor your meals is perfectly simple...

Whatever your ultimate kidney health goal is—improve kidney functions, lose weight, or simply eat healthier for your kidneys. Keeping food logs can help you do it.

With a diet that's as full of possible restrictions as a kidney diet (sodium, potassium, protein, and more...) food logs are among the best ways to get feedback from your dietitian. It's a simple solution that will help you achieve your goals.

Here are a couple of reasons why:

1. It holds you accountable.

By keeping track of your food, you are also keeping track of the choices you make about your diet. For many people, that's all the inspiration it takes to make better decisions about what to eat.

The majority of people will think twice about "cheating" on their renal diet, if they know they'll have to record what they actually ate.

What about omitting entries entirely? Sure, nothing can stop you from doing that. But if that's what you plan to do, then you might as well save yourself the trouble:

There's no point in simply PRETENDING to change. Only genuine effort will yield results.

2. It motivates you.

Food logging helps you remember and celebrate those small quotas. It's motivating to see your progress in a concrete form, even if it is just one small step at a time.

Your meal log is not only a record of what you ate—it's a list of your achievements, a catalog of all the good choices you make.

3. It helps you evaluate.

Sometimes, despite your best efforts, you don't always get the results you expect. When that happens, you need to take a step back and evaluate what you've been doing so far. But how can you do that if you don't have a record in the first place? And that's where your food logs come in.

With actual records to look over, you have a better chance of finding out what's wrong and figuring out how to correct it. And with those three reasons, we hope that you can see now why it's important to:

"Keep track of what you eat."

Creating a CKD-Friendly Meal Plan

This entire book may be a trove of valuable information on how to personalize your diet as a PERSONALIZED treatment and that can take you some time going back and forths and accomplishing a lot of things for you to finally master it.

But we can already start small!

What you need is a solution, a tool, that will help keep track of your diet: something that can help you track your progress and will give you insights as to what works and what doesn't work in helping your kidneys improve over time...and it's called a food journal.

If you are new to kidney dieting, having a food journal will help you stick to your diet plan. Hence, it can improve your kidney functions and prevent further kidney damage.

Most patients own a food journal to help them be more cautious and be more aware of their daily intake and to make sure that they are taking in the right amount of nutrients that boost your kidney health.

In totality, a food journal/diary looks like this:

Wk 9 Monday Food Plan		TOTAL DAILY INTAKE			
		Calories	Protein (g)	Carbs (g)	Fat (g)
		1159	190	79	78
Breakfast 7.00am	3 egg whites	48	11	0	0
	30g WPI (Biofurnace)	112	26	1	0
	30g raw rolled oats (complex carb)	113	3	17	3
Supplements: 1x Swisse Woman's Ultivite, 3x Fish oil 1500mg, 2 x Super Greens, 2 x Vitamin C 1000mg & 1 CLA					
Morning Snack	25g almonds	150	5	1	14
	1 Atkins Caram/Nut Chew Protein Bar	144	5	3	8
Pre Training 11.30am	130g Tuna in oil drained	277	31	0	17
	120g Salad Leaves with Beetroot	34	5	3	0
	1/2 cup brown rice	122	2	25	1
	10g Creatin (Biocharge)	42	7	0	0
Supplements: 4 x Super Greens, 1 CLA, 2 x Vitamin C 1000mg					
Weights 12.30pm	Back/Biceps/Abs (50 min)	-250			
	Treadmill inclined 4kmph (30min)	-150			
Post Training 2.00pm	30g WPI (Biofurnace)	112	26	1	0
	100g mixed berries	57	1	10	1
	1 cup skim milk	85	9	12	0
Dinner 5.30pm	150g Chicken Breast	248	47	0	5
	Green vegetables (1/2 cup broccoli, 50g beans, 6xasparagus)	64	8	3	1
	1/2 tbs olive oil + vinegar	80	0	0	9
Cardio 7.00pm	Zumba (60 min)	-350			
Before Bed 9.00pm	1 egg	71	6	0	5
	25g almonds	150	5	1	14
Supplements: 3 x Fish oil 1500mg, 4 x Super Greens, 2 x Vitamin C 1000mg & 1 CLA					

Important note: The image shown above is for illustration purposes only and differs from the food journal template provided on the annex section of this book (Page 179).

You have to diligently write down everything you eat and drink for every meal. By doing so, your dietitian can help you record specific details like calories, proteins, carbs, and fats that each food and beverage contains. The most important thing is that you have to be completely honest with yourself and your healthcare team as this can help you with your process and progress.

According to LiveStrong, an organization that has been supporting millions of people in pursuit of living healthy, keeping a food journal not only carries benefits such as keeping track of one's diet, but can also help you focus on your diet, and can help you attain and maintain your goals.

How do you keep a food journal?

Here are 5 steps on how to get started with food journaling:

STEP #1: SET UP YOUR JOURNAL

You will need to keep track of the following: date, time, place, item eaten, quantity consumed, and extra notes.

STEP #2: RECORD WHAT YOU EAT AND DRINK

Try to take note of everything that goes into your mouth. Be sure to include all meals, drinks, snacks, and even the small bites of food you eat while you cook.

Here are some important guidelines I teach my patients when starting kidney diet journaling:

- Be very specific when you record and break down complicated foods by ingredient. This will help you remember what the total amount of each nutrient is.
- All beverages should be recorded as well, especially the total water intake of the day. By doing so, this will give you an idea of whether or not you need to consume more water to help you stay hydrated.

STEP #3: WRITE DOWN ACCURATE AMOUNTS

Since you need to keep track of how much nutrients you need to consume in a day for your kidney condition, you have to write down the accurate quantities as this is important data.

I suggest you purchase a food scale or measuring cups to help confirm that the amounts are correct.

CKD Chef Duane TIP:

Take your favorite glass, bowl, or plate, and measure how much drink/food is in it!

That way, every time you use your favorite glass, you immediately know that it's 8 oz. of whatever you're drinking.

If you eat at a restaurant, you can check online if they have accurate quantities of the ingredients used in their serving sizes.

STEP #4: WRITE THE DATE, TIME, AND PLACE

By writing down the date, time, and place, you can find patterns in your eating habits. If you're making the necessary changes to your diet and lifestyle, this information may provide insight into why you eat specific foods at specific times. Or find out if you are dining out all too often in places that tend to go way above your salt recommendation.

STEP #5: RECORD YOUR FEELINGS AFTER EATING.

It is also important that you jot down notes on how a food or meal makes you feel. After eating, wait 10-20 minutes to assess how you feel. It takes approximately 20 minutes for the body to know that you're satisfied.

Don't forget to also include any physical symptoms or side effects after eating. For example, you may notice that you have an upset stomach after eating dairy products.

Once you have done these 5 steps, you can then analyze your data after a specific period of time.

Recording everything you eat and drink provides regulation and accountability for what you put in your mouth and it can provide valuable insight for your doctor of what you eat. With this, it can also point out if you need more variety.

For example, if you need to eat more vegetables, or more meat, and less processed food. It can also lead to decreased caloric intake and can help you lose weight at the same time, too.

In addition, it will reveal if you are eating larger portions than your daily requirement. If you continue to keep track of your daily consumption for an extended period of time, you will start to notice the changes in your food intake and you will be able to monitor the progress you have made towards reaching your goal. After all, it's not about the data that you get. It's about the actions you do with those data. Don't you agree?

Just a little assignment for you so you can begin by starting small. Using the food diary on the annex section (page 179), try starting to record your meal starting today for one full week.

Understanding Portion Sizes

One thing you need to learn, in the case of renal diet nutrition, is to portion your food. Finding the right size of food servings for you will greatly help in regulating the amount of nutrients and wastes your kidneys filter.

Which leads me to my first question: *How much should you eat?*

Controlling what you eat is a vital step in achieving great results in following a renal diet. Your kidneys will find it easier to filter off your wastes if you don't eat more than what's necessary.

Also, a balance between the calories you eat and the ones you burn is one of the secrets to keep a healthy weight. The less sedentary you go (I'll discuss this in another chapter), the more calories you offset.

Picture this: a 120-pound man who burns a lot of calories through intense physical activity several times a week may need to eat more calories, than a man of similar size but mostly inactive and goes for a short walk once a week.

Portion Distortion

A study published in 2012 found that 96% of restaurant meals exceed USDA recommendations for fat, salt, and overall calories.

That's mainly due to the fact that restaurant and fast food chains are now serving food in gigantic plates, big cups, and king-sized packages. This is also part of the reason why fast foods are part of restrictions in a renal diet.

Another study found that modern portion sizes of popular foods added *an extra 50-150 calories*. Let's take an example:

Coffee (20 years ago)	**Coffee** (today)

WITH WHOLE MILK AND SUGAR

MOCHA COFFEE
(WITH STEAMED WHOLE MILK AND MOCHA SYRUP)

8 OUNCES

45 CALORIES

16 OUNCES

350 CALORIES

That's a difference of 305 calories!

A 130 pound person would need to walk for an hour and 20 minutes to get rid of that many calories.

Luckily, there are certain fast foods you can enjoy, with <u>a few modifications to your order</u>, of course.

Portion Size vs Serving Size

Basically...

SERVING SIZE - the recommended amount of food, as stated on the product's food label.

PORTION SIZE - the amount of food you choose to eat at one time, whether you're at home or in a restaurant.

Sometimes, the serving size matches the portion size, but it most often will be up to you. To help you decide for your renal diet, here's a serving size guide you can use. So, here is a food portioning hack chart to help you easily remember how to adjust food portions on your plate.

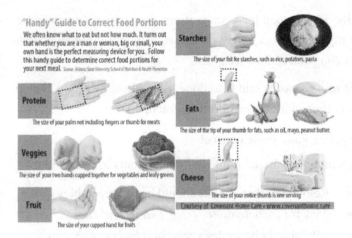

"Handy" Guide to Correct Food Portions

We often know what to eat but not how much. It turns out that whether you are a man or woman, big or small, your own hand is the perfect measuring device for you. Follow this handy guide to determine correct food portions for your next meal. *Source: Arizona State University School of Nutrition & Health Promotion*

Protein — The size of your palm not including fingers or thumb for meats

Veggies — The size of your two hands cupped together for vegetables and leafy greens

Fruit — The size of your cupped hand for fruits

Starches — The size of your fist for starches, such as rice, potatoes, pasta

Fats — The size of the tip of your thumb for fats, such as oil, mayo, peanut butter.

Cheese — The size of your entire thumb is one serving

Courtesy of Covenant Home Care • www.covenanthome.care

Properly portioning your food will give your body time to digest the food effectively, allowing better absorption of nutrients and reducing the amount of waste that your kidneys have to filter.

If you want to optimize your kidney functions, then I suggest you learn the charts above by heart. You can put it somewhere in your kitchen or dining area for easy reference! That way, you will be able to commit them into memory effectively. This will really help you determine if you are eating the proper amount of food. And I want you to practice this in your next meal. It may take a while for you to get it, but with practice, the habit will surely stick and the benefits you're going to get will be spectacular.

First, your body will be so used to eating small portions, that it will condition your body to become full just by eating small.

Second, most people will eventually feel better and will have more energy to do things once they have eaten moderate portions compared to how they used to eat.

73

Finally, if you monitor your portions properly, it can improve your digestion process. By doing so, it is more effective even when you want to lose weight.

But it sounds easier said than done, right? Don't worry, I'll help you get there with these 3 Portion Practice Tips:

1. Practice your plate control

Take a plate and divide it into 3 compartments in your mind:

- Remember that… 50% should be for vegetables
- 25% for carbohydrates *(rice, beans, and etc.)*
- 25% should be for lean protein *(chicken, fish, etc)*.

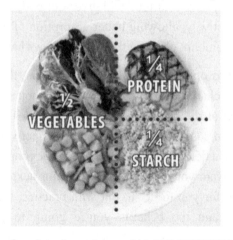

Image from: *https://www.pinterest.ph/pin/298152437809682150/*

For protein, if you remember from our lesson where we presented a food that's high on Protein and replaced them with ones that are lower and kidney-friendlier, the portion size of each food item was 100g.

So, how much is 100 grams? If you've never had to think about this before, that's perfectly normal. One of the most surprising things is starting to be conscious of the amount of food you are eating – especially when it comes to your favorites. The best thing to do is to actually get a kitchen weighing scale and measure the food that makes up your usual meals.

The second best thing to do is to always look at the nutrition labels because it specifies how many grams/ml there is of the food you are getting.

IF you also have to follow a protein-restricted diet, you should make it a point to calculate the protein portion in your meals. Small changes you can do to portion control:

- Eat more of things that are low-protein. Adding more of the good stuff tends to be easier than removing the bad stuff.
- If you absolutely have to have a high-protein food, then eat a smaller portion. Choose half a pork chop instead of a whole. Instead of a big homemade meatball, make smaller meatballs and use only half the portion. Take just the drumstick instead of a whole chicken leg.

2. Don't "Super Size" it

There's a reason why the Super Size Me documentary struck such a nerve – bigger portions are not always better, especially when it comes to a CKD diet. An article points out how since the 1970s, American food portions have grown as much as 138%!

Whether we are really hungry or not, the more food that is put in front of us, the more food we end up eating.

Just like the example on portion distortion earlier, you must keep in mind the calories (and sodium!) that you will be consuming. It's also a bad cycle: by eating a lot, your stomach gets used to expecting more food, so you find yourself to be hungry sooner... which urges you to eat more.

3. Take a look at labels

The Nutrition Facts Label is that friend you can count on to always tell you what you need to hear. It helps you determine what an appropriate portion should be for you. And based on the nutrients, steer you towards eating healthier and aim for more kidney-friendly foods.

Nutrition Facts

2 servings per container

Serving size 1 cup (140g)

Amount per serving

Calories 160

	% Daily Value*
Total Fat 8g	10%
Saturated Fat 3g	15%
Trans Fat 0g	
Cholesterol 0mg	0%
Sodium 60mg	3%
Total Carbohydrate 21g	8%
Dietary Fiber 3g	11%
Total Sugars 15g	
Includes 5g Added Sugars	10%
Protein 3g	
Vitamin D 5mcg	25%
Calcium 20mg	2%
Iron 1mg	6%
Potassium 230mg	4%

*The % Daily Value tells you how much a nutrient in a serving of food contributes to a daily diet. 2000 calories a day is used for general nutrition advice.

CKD-Friendly Recipes

As I have promised in the beginning, I cannot just keep on babbling about the basics, the fun-facts, and the truths about kidney dieting without sharing with you some recipe ideas that I have shared with my patients before.

However, though these recipes are created by a Nutritionist Dietitian for CKD patients, it is still best to consult your own dietitian in terms of your diet restrictions and needs. I have included the macronutrient and micronutrients summary in there to make it extra easy for you.

Breakfast Ideas

Easy Stir Fry Cabbage

🕐 **15 min** 🍽 **4 servings** *230 Kcal / serving* *9g Protein* *9g Fat* *39g Carbs*

INGREDIENTS

Vegetable broth, 100 ml (100 g)
Bell pepper, 1 (100 g)
Spring onions, 1 tbsp chopped (6 g)
Olive oil, 1 ounce (28 g)
Garlic, 2 cloves (6 g)
Cabbage, 1 head, medium (about 5-3/4" dia) (908 g)
Soy sauce, 2 tbsp (36 g)
Bell peppers, 2 (238 g)
Ground pepper, 1 tsp (2 g)
Onion, 1 medium size (150 g)
Paprika, 1/2 teaspoon (1 g)
Oyster mushroom sauce, 2 tbsp (100 g)

Instructions

1. Core and shred the cabbage into pieces, wash and dry well; set it aside.

2. Heat a wok over high heat, add the oil, and saute onion slices and minced garlic for a minute.

3. Toss in bell peppers, shredded cabbage and continue sauteing for 4 minutes stirring occasionally.

4. Add vegetable broth, soy sauce, and oyster mushroom sauce and mix well.

5. Continue tossing for another 3 minutes until the cabbage has wilted.

6. Season with smoked paprika, ground black pepper, and salt, and garnish with chopped spring onions and serve immediately.*Source: https://simplybakings.com/easy-stir-fry-cabbage*

MACRONUTRIENT SUMMARY

	TOTAL	PER 100 G	PER SERVING
Energy (kCal)	921.7	50.6	230.4
Protein (g)	34.3	1.9	8.6
Fat (g)	33.8	1.9	8.5
Carbs (g)	157	8.6	39.3
Fiber (g)	59.6	3.3	14.9

MICRONUTRIENT SUMMARY

	TOTAL	PER 100 G	PER SERVING
Sugars (g)	48.9	2.7	12.2
Fiber (g)	59.6	3.3	14.9
Calcium, Ca (mg)	910.8	50	227.7
Iron, Fe (mg)	18.7	1	4.7
Magnesium, Mg (mg)	367.4	20.2	91.9
Phosphorus, P (mg)	274	15.0	68.5
Potassium, K (mg)	2263	124	565.75
Sodium, Na (mg)	1245	68.21	311.25
Zinc, Zn (mg)	4.9	0.3	1.2
Vitamin D (ug)	0.7	0	0.2
Vitamin C (mg)	725.5	39.9	181.9
Cholesterol (mg)	0	0	0

Cauliflower Rice and Lentils

🕐 **25 min** 🍽 **2 servings** *155 Kcal / serving 6g Protein 8g Fat 18g Carbs*

INGREDIENTS

Vegetable broth, 1/4 cup (47.1 g)
Oregano, 1 teaspoon (2 g)
Celery, 1/4 cup (21.3 g)
Carrots, 1/4 cup (30.8 g)
Olive oil, 1 servings (14 g)
Onion, 1/4 cup (38.5 g)
Lentils, 1/2 cup (99 g)
Cauliflower rice, 1/2 cup (80 g)
Garlic Powder, 1 teaspoon (3 g)
Pepper, 1/4 tsp (0.5 g)

Instructions

Heat the olive oil in a large skillet over medium heat.

Add the onion, celery, and carrots to the skillet and cook until softened, about 5 minutes.

Add the cauliflower rice and vegetable broth and cook for an additional 5 minutes.

Stir in the cooked lentils, garlic powder, oregano, and black pepper. Cook for an additional 5 minutes, stirring occasionally, until the cauliflower rice is cooked through.

Serve hot.

Comments

You can replace/ substitute lentils with preferred plant-based protein

Additionally, the same goes with substitution of vegetables to other low potassium ones.

MACRONUTRIENT SUMMARY

	TOTAL	PER 100 G	PER SERVING
Energy (kCal)	309.3	92	154.7
Protein (g)	12.2	3.5	6.1
Fat (g)	14.9	4.4	7.5
Carbs (g)	35.4	10.5	17.7
Fiber (g)	12.5	3.7	6.3

MICRONUTRIENT SUMMARY

	TOTAL	PER 100 G	PER SERVING
Sugars (g)	7.1	2.1	3.6
Fiber (g)	12.5	3.7	6.3
Calcium, Ca (mg)	102	30.3	51
Iron, Fe (mg)	4.9	1.5	2.5
Magnesium, Mg (mg)	66.6	19.8	33.3
Phosphorus, P (mg)	258	75.8	129
Potassium, K (mg)	891.6	265.3	445.8
Sodium, Na (mg)	211.2	62.8	105.6
Zinc, Zn (mg)	1.8	0.5	0.9
Vitamin D (ug)	0	0	0
Vitamin C (mg)	45.6	13.6	22.8
Cholesterol (mg)	0	0	0

Stir-Fry Tofu

🕐 *25 min* 🍲: *4 servings*   *464 Kcal / serving 15g Protein 32g Fat 36g Carbs*

INGREDIENTS

Hoisin sauce, 4 Tbsp
Shiitake mushrooms, 2 ounces (56.7 g)
Snow peas, 1 oz (113.4 g)
Sesame oil, 1 dash (2 g)
Vegetable oil, 100 grams (100 g)
Garlic, 3 cloves (9 g)
Soy sauce, 1 tsp
Extra tofu, 16 ounce (453.6 g)
Cornstarch, 2 tsp (4 g)
Brown sugar, 1 tablespoon (12 g)
Salt and pepper, to taste
Onions, 1 portion (100 g)
Pepper Flakes, 1 tsp (100 g)
Rice Vinegar, 1 tablespoon (16 g)

Instructions

1. In a medium-sized bowl, add soy sauce, rice black vinegar, brown sugar, cornstarch, red pepper flakes, and mix until combined, set aside.
2. Heat a large pan on medium heat with oil and fry the tofu until all sides are golden, then remove, transfer to a plate lined with paper towels, and set aside.
3. Add the remaining oil into the same pan and saute sliced red onions and crushed garlic cloves for about 1 minute.
4. Add slices of mushrooms and continue cooking for 3 minutes on medium-high heat.
5. Stir in the snow peas and cook for 2 minutes.
6. Add the fried tofu and the soy sauce mixture.
7. Cover and allow it to steam for 2 minutes on medium-low heat.
8. Add hoisin sauce and adjust the seasoning.
9. Turn off the heat and add a touch of sesame oil.
10. Serve with steamed Jasmin Rice.

Source: https://simplybakings.com/tofu-stir-fry-with-snow-peas/

MACRONUTRIENT SUMMARY

	TOTAL	PER 100 G	PER SERVING
Energy (kCal)	1854.6	169.2	463.7
Protein (g)	59.5	5.4	14.9
Fat (g)	129	11.8	32.3
Carbs (g)	144.6	13.2	36.2
Fiber (g)	44.6	4.1	11.2

MICRONUTRIENT SUMMARY

	TOTAL	PER 100 G	PER SERVING
Sugars (g)	61.3	5.6	15.3
Fiber (g)	44.6	4.1	11.2
Calcium, Ca (mg)	608.7	55.5	152.2
Iron, Fe (mg)	27.5	2.5	6.9
Magnesium, Mg (mg)	359.2	32.8	89.8
Phosphorus, P (mg)	766	69.95	191.5
Potassium, K (mg)	1694	154.70	423.50
Sodium, Na (mg)	2027	185.11	506.75
Zinc, Zn (mg)	8.6	0.8	2.2
Vitamin D (ug)	0.2	0	0.1
Vitamin C (mg)	79.3	7.2	19.8
Cholesterol (mg)	3	0.3	0.8

Lunch and Dinner Ideas

Cauliflower Crust Pizza

🕐 *45 min* 🍽 *4 servings*   *143 Kcal / serving 11g Protein 8g Fat 9g Carbs*

INGREDIENTS

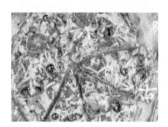

Parmesan, 1/2 cup (48.5 g)
Mozzarella, 1/4 cup (29.3 g)
Egg, 1 medium (51 g)
Dried basil, 1/2 teaspoon (0.5 g)
Oregano, 1 teaspoon (3 g)
Arugula, 2/3 cup (13.3 g)
Mushrooms, 1/2 cup (46.5 g)
Pepperoni, 5 piece (10 g)
cauliflower rice, 3 cups (480 g)
marinara sauce, 61.3 g
Cherry Tomatoes, 4 100 gram (68 g)

Instructions

Pre-heat oven to 425 F
(If youre using a pizza stone, place it in the oven now)
Place the cauliflower rice in a large microwave safe bowl and
microwave on high for 3-5 minutes. Allow to cool in bowl.
When the cauliflower is cool, add the parmesan, egg and optional
herbs. Mix well until a dough forms.
Line an oven tray with parchment paper and form a circle with the
dough, creating a raised lip around the edges.
Bake in preheated oven for 20 minutes. Remove from oven and
spread marinara sauce evenly on top of the crust.
Sprinkle with grated mozzarella followed by desired toppings.
Bake again for 10 minutes, or until the cheese melts. Slice and serve
hot.

Source: https://lifemadesweeter.com/cauliflower-crust-pizza

MACRONUTRIENT SUMMARY

	TOTAL	PER 100 G	PER SERVING
Energy (kCal)	570.8	70.4	142.7
Protein (g)	44.9	5.5	11.2
Fat (g)	30.5	3.8	7.6
Carbs (g)	36.8	4.5	9.2
Fiber (g)	13.1	1.6	3.3

MICRONUTRIENT SUMMARY

	TOTAL	PER 100 G	PER SERVING
Sugars (g)	15.2	1.9	3.8
Fiber (g)	13.1	1.6	3.3
Calcium, Ca (mg)	955.9	117.8	239
Iron, Fe (mg)	6.6	0.8	1.7
Magnesium, Mg (mg)	144.5	17.8	36.1
Phosphorus, P (mg)	856.4	105.6	214.1
Potassium, K (mg)	2178	268.4	544.5
Sodium, Na (mg)	1530.2	188.6	382.6
Zinc, Zn (mg)	5	0.6	1.3
Vitamin D (ug)	1.6	0.2	0.4
Vitamin C (mg)	254.2	31.3	63.6
Cholesterol (mg)	255.5	31.5	63.9

Quick Easy Fish Stew

🕐 **30 min** 🍴 **4 servings** *440 Kcal / serving 36g Protein 24g Fat 17gCarbs*

INGREDIENTS

Thyme, 1 pinch (0.1 g)
Oregano, 1 pinch (0.1 g)
Salt, 1 tsp
Canned tomatoes, 1/2 cup (116.3 g)
Onion, 1 1/2 cup (236.8 g)
Wine, 1/2 cup (113.5 g)
Clam juice, 4 ounces (226.8 g)
Pepper, 4 servings (0.4 g)
Parsley, 2/3 cup (39.2 g)
Garlic cloves, 3 (9 g)
Extra virgin olive oil, 6 tablespoon (84 g)
Tomato paste, 2 teaspoons (12 g)
Fish fillets, 1 1/2 lb (671.4 g)
Tabasco sauce, 1/8 teaspoon (0.4 g)

Instructions

1. Heat olive oil in a large thick-bottomed pot over medium-high heat.
2. Add onion and sauté 4 minutes, add the garlic and cook a minute more.
3. Add parsley and stir 2 minutes.
4. Add tomato and tomato paste, and gently cook for 10 minutes or so.
5. Add clam juice, dry white wine, and Bsh. Tring to a simmer and simmer until the Fish is cooked through and easily flakes apart, about 3 to 5 minutes.
6. Add seasoning (oregano, thyme, Tabasco).
7. Add salt and pepper to taste. Ladle into bowls and serve.
8. Great served with crusty bread for dipping in the fish stew broth.

Source: https://www.simplyrecipes.com/recipes/dads_fish_stew

MACRONUTRIENT SUMMARY

	TOTAL	PER 100 G	PER SERVING
Energy (kCal)	1758.7	116.3	439.7
Protein (g)	143.1	9.5	35.8
Fat (g)	96.9	6.4	24.2
Carbs (g)	65.9	4.4	16.5
Fiber (g)	9.3	0.6	2.3

MICRONUTRIENT SUMMARY

	TOTAL	PER 100 G	PER SERVING
Sugars (g)	24.6	1.6	6.2
Fiber (g)	9.3	0.6	2.3
Calcium, Ca (mg)	259.4	17.2	64.9
Iron, Fe (mg)	9.6	0.6	2.4
Magnesium, Mg (mg)	267.7	17.7	66.9
Phosphorus, P (mg)	1319.7	87.3	329.9
Potassium, K (mg)	3300.2	218.3	825.1
Sodium, Na (mg)	2301.3	152.2	575.3
Zinc, Zn (mg)	3.7	0.2	0.9
Vitamin D (ug)	20.8	1.4	5.2
Vitamin C (mg)	97.6	6.5	24.4
Cholesterol (mg)	335.7	22.2	83.9

Chicken Pelau

🕐 **60 min**   ⊘ **4 servings**   *653 Kcal / serving*   *36g Protein*   31g *Fat*   57g *Carbs*

INGREDIENTS

boneless skinless chicken thighs, target stores, 6 serving (672 g)
Onion, Fresh, 1 medium (105.8 g)
Ginger, fresh, 1 tbsp (20 g)
Lime juice, fresh, 1/2 ounce (14.2 g)
peeled garlic cloves, 2 clove (8 g)
Coriander (cilantro) leaves, raw, 1/4 cup (4 g)
Parsley, 1 tablespoons (5 g)
Chives, 1 tsp chopped (1 g)
Spices, oregano, dried, 1 teaspoon (3 g)
Spices, thyme, dried, 1 teaspoon (2 g)
TABASCO PEPPERS PEPPER SAUCE, 1 serving (5 g)
Oil, olive, salad or cooking, 3 tbsp (42 g)
Sugars, brown, 3 tbsp (3k g)
Pigeon peas (red gram), mature seeds, cooked, boiled, without salt, 1 cup (168 g)
Carrots, raw, 1 portion (61.6 g)
Peppers, sweet, red, raw, 1 medium (k3 g)
Celery, raw, 1 stalk (44 g)
Tomato, Fresh, 1 small (k5 g)
Worcestershire sauce, 1 tsp (5 g)
coconut cream, thai agri foods co., ltd., 1 serving (k0 g)
Rice, white, long-grain, parboiled, unenriched, cooked, 2 cup (316 g)
Table salt, 1 teaspoon (5 g)
Black Pepper, 1/2 tsp, ground (1.2 g)
Water, 3 portion(s) (630 g)

Instructions

1. Marinate the chicken pieces with the seasoning/marinade above for a few hours or overnight.

2. When ready to cook, heat a large pot on high heat and add oil. When the oil is hot, add the brown sugar. Don't stir yet. Let it melt and start to get dark brown around the dome of the edges. Don't let it burn.
3. Start adding the seasoned chicken, a few pieces at a time, stirring to ensure all the pieces get coated evenly with the caramelized/burnt sugar. Don't add the seasoning from the bowl yet. You will add that later.
4. After adding all the chicken pieces, cover the pot and allow to cook on medium heat for about 10 minutes. Stir up a few times to get all the pieces well covered. This will create some liquid from the chicken.
5. Then open he pot lid, turn up the heat for about 3-5 minutes to allow the chicken to get a nice brown color.
6. Add the drained cooked pigeon peas. Stir. Cover pot with lid for about a couple more minutes.
7. Now you can add any seasoning that was left over the marinated chicken bowl
8. Add onion, hot pepper and/or pimiento, carrot and/or pumpkin, bell peppers, and tomato.
9. Add about ¼ cup of water if needed and cover the pot to help them cook a little – maybe 3 – 4 minutes.
10. Add the ketchup, Worcestershire sauce, salt and pepper.
11. Then add the 3 cups of water and mix all together.
12. Add the soaked and drained rice and stir well. Turn the heat to high to bring to a boil.
13 Then run the heat to very low, cover the pot and simmer for about 30 to 35 minutes, checking periodically to ensure it's not sticking to the bottom of the pot. Taste and adjust seasoning as needed.
14. After you turn the heat off, add some fresh parsley if you want and mix it in with you pelau. Finely chopped celery leaves also works well.

MACRONUTRIENT SUMMARY

	TOTAL	PER 100 G	PER SERVING
Energy (kCal)	2611.8	101.7	653
Protein (g)	143.2	5.6	35.8
Fat (g)	125.3	4.9	31.3
Carbs (g)	226.1	8.8	56.5
Fiber (g)	25.3	1	6.3

MICRONUTRIENT SUMMARY

	TOTAL	PER 100 G	PER SERVING
Sugars (g)	83.9	3.3	21
Fiber (g)	25.3	1	6.3
Calcium, Ca (mg)	365.7	14.2	91.4
Iron, Fe (mg)	15.3	0.6	3.8
Magnesium, Mg (mg)	200.7	7.8	50.2
Phosphorus, P (mg)	944	36.68	236
Potassium, K (mg)	2838	110.29	709.50
Sodium, Na (mg)	2665	103.57	666.25
Zinc, Zn (mg)	4	0.2	1
Vitamin D (ug)	0	0	0
Vitamin C (mg)	163.6	6.4	40.9
Cholesterol (mg)	631.7	24.6	157.9

Double Tomato Pesto Spaghetti with Zucchini Noodles

⏱ 30 min   🍴 4 servings   454 *Kcal / serving*   *13g Protein*   *22g Fat*   *55g Carbs*

INGREDIENTS

Basil leaves, 1/2 cup (12 g)
Lemon zest, 1/2 tsp (1 g)
Lemon juice, 1 tablespoons (15 g)
Salt, 1/4 teaspoon (1.8 g)
Olive oil, 2 servings (28 g)
Zucchini, 1 large (324 g)
Garlic cloves, 2 clove (6 g)
Walnuts, 2/3 cup (76.7 g)
Oil packed sun dried tomatoes, 1/4 cup (28.8 g)
bell pepper, 4 medium (298 g)
nutritional yeast, 1 teaspoons (4 g)
red pepper flakes, 1/4 teaspoon (0.5 g)
spaghetti, 1/2 lb (226.8 g)

Instructions

1. Bring a large pot of salted water to boil for the spaghetti. Cook the pasta until al dente, according to package directions. Drain and transfer to a large serving bowl.
2. Spiralize the zucchini with a spiralizer, or turn the zucchini into noodles with a julienne peeler, or grate the zucchini the long way on a large box grater.
3. Toast the walnuts: In a medium skillet over medium heat, cook the walnuts, stirring occasionally, until they smell nice and fragrant, about 7 minutes. Set aside to cool.
4. Cook the cherry tomatoes: In a large saucepan over medium-high heat, combine the cherry tomatoes, olive oil and a pinch of salt. Cover the pot and cook, stirring occasionally, until the tomatoes have burst open and they are cooking in their own juices, about 7 to 8 minutes. Set aside.
5. In a food processor, combine the walnuts, half of the cooked tomatoes, sun-dried tomatoes, garlic, lemon zest, 1 tablespoon lemon juice, red pepper flakes, teaspoon salt and several twists of freshly ground black pepper. Blend until the mixture is pretty smooth, then season to taste with additional lemon

91

6. juice, salt and/or pepper until the flavors really sing. Blend again.
7. Pour the pesto over the spaghetti and toss to combine. If you'll be consuming this dish in one sitting, go ahead and toss in all of the zucchini noodles now,
8. too. (If you plan on having leftovers, store the zucchini noodles separately from the rest, as they leach water when they're exposed to salt. I just pile the noodles on top of my individual bowls and wait to stir them in when I'm ready to eat). Pour the rest of the cherry tomatoes on top of the dish, and sprinkle the basil over them. Toss gently, and divide the mixture into bowls. Top individual bowls with Parmesan or nutritional yeast, if you'd like, and a light drizzle of olive oil. Serve immediately.

MACRONUTRIENT SUMMARY

	TOTAL	PER 100 G	PER SERVING
Energy (kCal)	1816	177.5	454
Protein (g)	52.5	5.1	13.1
Fat (g)	87.8	8.6	22
Carbs (g)	220	21.15	55
Fiber (g)	25.2	2.5	6.3

MICRONUTRIENT SUMMARY

	TOTAL	PER 100 G	PER SERVING
Sugars (g)	29.2	2.9	7.3
Fiber (g)	25.2	2.5	6.3
Calcium, Ca (mg)	245.7	24	61.4
Iron, Fe (mg)	9.4	0.9	2.4
Magnesium, Mg (mg)	369.7	36.2	92.4
Phosphorus, P (mg)	953.2	93.2	238.3
Potassium, K (mg)	2934.9	287	733.7
Sodium, Na (mg)	818.2	80	204.6
Zinc, Zn (mg)	7.8	0.8	2
Vitamin D (ug)	0	0	0
Vitamin C (mg)	480.8	47	120.2
Cholesterol (mg)	0	0	0

Curried Butternut Squash Soup

🕐 **30 min**   ☕ **4 servings**   541 *Kcal / serving*   *16g Protein*   27g *Fat*   72g *Carbs*

INGREDIENTS

Vegetable broth, 100 ml (100 g)
Shallots), 2 (50 g)
Garlic, 2 (6 g)
Curry powder, 1 jar (100 g)
Butternut squash , 1 portion(s) (100 g)
Avocado oil, 1 tbsp (14 g)
Full-fat coconut milk, 1 ml (1 g)
Pumpkin seeds, 1 portion(s) (100 g)
Sea salt, 1 serving (100 g)
Ground cinnamon, 1 tsp (0.7 g)
Maple syrup), 1 tbsp (100 g)
Chili garlic paste, 1 teaspoon (100 g)
Coconut milk, 14 ounce (396.9 g)

Instructions

1. Heat a large pot over medium heat.
2. Once hot, add oil, shallots, and garlic. Sauté for 2 minutes, stirring frequently.
3. Add butternut squash and season with salt, pepper, curry powder, and ground cinnamon. Stir to coat. Then cover and cook for 4 minutes, stirring occasionally.
4. Add coconut milk, vegetable broth, maple syrup or coconut sugar, and chili garlic paste (optional - for heat).
5. Bring to a low boil over medium heat and then reduce heat to low, cover, and simmer for 15 minutes or until butternut squash is fork tender.
6. Use an immersion blender, or transfer soup to a blender, and purée on high until creamy and smooth. If using a blender, return soup back to pot.
7. Taste and adjust seasonings, adding more curry powder, salt, or sweetener as needed. Continue cooking for a few more minutes over medium heat.

8. Serve as is or with garnishes of choice (options above). Store leftovers covered in the refrigerator for 3-4 days or in the freezer up to 1 month. Best when fresh.

Comments
You can upgrade nutritionally by adding greens, such as, chopped spinach, moringa leaves, boiled/ chopped broccoli
Source: https://minimalistbaker.com/curried-butternut-squash-soup/

MACRONUTRIENT SUMMARY

	TOTAL	PER 100 G	PER SERVING
Energy (kCal)	2164	185.2	541
Protein (g)	64.2	5.5	16.1
Fat (g)	107.7	9.2	26.9
Carbs (g)	287.4	24.6	71.9
Fiber (g)	90.7	7.8	22.7

MICRONUTRIENT SUMMARY

	TOTAL	PER 100 G	PER SERVING
Sugars (g)	77.8	6.7	19.5
Fiber (g)	90.7	7.8	22.7
Calcium, Ca (mg)	1282.1	109.7	320.5
Iron, Fe (mg)	40.9	3.5	10.2
Magnesium, Mg (mg)	1090.9	93.4	272.7
Phosphorus, P (mg)	1987.6	170.1	496.9
Potassium, K (mg)	4277.1	366	1069.3
Sodium, Na (mg)	936.9	80.2	234.2
Zinc, Zn (mg)	15.3	1.3	3.8
Vitamin D (ug)	0	0	0
Vitamin C (mg)	61.1	5.2	15.3
Cholesterol (mg)	0	0	0

Cauliflower Risotto with Brie and Almonds

🕐 45 min   ⊘ 4 servings   596 *Kcal / serving*   *17g Protein*   *27g Fat*   *69g Carbs*

INGREDIENTS

Thyme sprigs, 3 handful (6 g)
Unsalted butter, 1 tablespoon (14 g)
Vegetable broth, 4 cups (784 g)
Brie, 5 ounces (145 g)
Cauliflower, 1/2 head (276.5 g)
Olive oil, 2 servings (28 g)
Almonds, 1/3 cup (49.7 g)
Water, 2 1/2 cup (587.5 g)
Dry White Wine, 1/3 cup (83.3 g)
arborio rice, 1 cups (300 g)

Instructions

1. Bring broth, water, and thyme sprigs to a bare simmer in a medium saucepan.
2. Meanwhile, heat butter and 1 tablespoon oil in a 4-quart heavy saucepan over medium-high heat until foam subsides, then sauté cauliflower with ¼ teaspoon salt until crisp-tender and golden brown, about 6 minutes.
3. Add thyme leaves and sauté 1 minute.
4. Transfer to a bowl. Add remaining tablespoon oil to pan, then add rice
5. and cook, stirring constantly, 1 minute.
6. Add wine and simmer briskly, stirring, until wine has been absorbed,
7. about 1 minute.
   Add 1/2 cup hot broth and briskly simmer, stirring, until broth has been absorbed. Continue simmering and adding hot broth, about 1/2 cup at a time, stirring constantly and waiting until each addition has been absorbed before adding the next, until rice is just tender and looks creamy, 18 to 22 minutes. (There will be leftover broth.)
8. Stir in cauliflower, Brie, and salt and pepper to taste.

9. Thin with some of remaining broth if desired. Serve topped with almonds.

   Source: https://www.epicurious.com/recipes/food/views/cauliflower-risotto-with-Brie-and-Almonds-350559

MACRONUTRIENT SUMMARY

	TOTAL	PER 100 G	PER SERVING
Energy (kCal)	2384.3	104.9	596.1
Protein (g)	67.7	3	16.9
Fat (g)	107.3	4.7	26.8
Carbs (g)	274.2	12.1	68.6
Fiber (g)	21	0.9	5.3

MICRONUTRIENT SUMMARY

	TOTAL	PER 100 G	PER SERVING
Sugars (g)	13.4	0.6	3.4
Fiber (g)	21	0.9	5.3
Calcium, Ca (mg)	546.8	24	136.7
Iron, Fe (mg)	18.5	0.8	4.6
Magnesium, Mg (mg)	305.5	13.4	76.4
Phosphorus, P (mg)	819	49.69	204.75
Potassium, K (mg)	1373	83.3	343.25
Sodium, Na (mg)	2402	145.75	600.5
Zinc, Zn (mg)	9.6	0.4	2.4
Vitamin D (ug)	0.7	0	0.2
Vitamin C (mg)	146	6.4	36.5
Cholesterol (mg)	175.1	7.7	43.8

Snack Ideas and Healthy Desserts

Almond Berry Smoothie

🕐 10 min ⊘ 1 servings   305 *Kcal / serving*   6g *Protein*   11g *Fat*   52g *Carbs*

INGREDIENTS

Banana, 1 medium (7" to 7-7/8" long) (118 g)
Blueberries, 1 cup (148 g)
Water, 1 serving (236.6 g)
Almond butter, 1 tbsp (16 g)
Almond milk, 1/2 cup (125 g)

Instructions

1. Combine blueberries, banana, almond milk, and almond butter in a blender; blend until smooth, adding water
for a thinner smoothie.

Source: https://www.allrecipes.com/recipe/246613/almond-berry-smoothie/

MACRONUTRIENT SUMMARY

	TOTAL	PER 100 G	PER SERVING
Energy (kCal)	305.1	47.4	305.1
Protein (g)	6.4	1	6.4
Fat (g)	11.3	1.8	11.3
Carbs (g)	51.9	8.1	51.9
Fiber (g)	8.6	1.3	8.6

MICRONUTRIENT SUMMARY

	TOTAL	PER 100 G	PER SERVING
Sugars (g)	30	4.7	30
Fiber (g)	8.6	1.3	8.6
Calcium, Ca (mg)	227.4	35.3	227.4
Iron, Fe (mg)	1.3	0.2	1.3
Magnesium, Mg (mg)	87.7	13.6	87.7
Phosphorus, P (mg)	125	19.4	125
Potassium, K (mg)	656.1	101.9	656.1
Sodium, Na (mg)	178.1	27.7	178.1
Zinc, Zn (mg)	1	0.2	1
Vitamin D (ug)	0	0	0
Vitamin C (mg)	24.6	3.8	24.6
Cholesterol (mg)	0	0	0

Oatmeal Cookies

⏱ 41 min   🍪 24 servings   12*Kcal / serving*   *1g Protein*   *0g Fat*   3*g Carbs*

INGREDIENTS

Vanilla extract, 1 tsp (5 g)
Applesauce (Mott's LLP), 1 serving (123 g)
Salt, table, 1 teaspoon (5 g)
Oat bran, raw, 1 cup (94 g)

Instructions

1. Preheat oven to 200F
2. Mix all ingredients in a bowl
3. Scoop out 1 tablespoon dough and shape into balls
4. Prepare baking sheets lined with parchment paper and press cookie balls on the baking sheet to flatten a bit
5. Bake in the oven for 10 to 15 minutes or until cookies look golden.
6. Cool in a cooling rack for at least 10 minutes before eating.

MACRONUTRIENT SUMMARY

	TOTAL	PER 100 G	PER SERVING
Energy (kCal)	296.1	130.4	12.3
Protein (g)	16.3	7.2	0.7
Fat (g)	6.6	2.9	0.3
Carbs (g)	76.9	33.9	3.2
Fiber (g)	15.5	6.8	0.6

MICRONUTRIENT SUMMARY

	TOTAL	PER 100 G	PER SERVING
Sugars (g)	14	6.2	0.6
Fiber (g)	15.5	6.8	0.6
Calcium, Ca (mg)	56.3	24.8	2.3
Iron, Fe (mg)	5.1	2.2	0.2
Magnesium, Mg (mg)	221.16	97.6	9.2
Phosphorus, P (mg)	690.3	304.1	28.8
Potassium, K (mg)	629.6	277.4	26.2
Sodium, Na (mg)	1942.1	855.6	80.9
Zinc, Zn (mg)	2.9	1.3	0.1
Vitamin D (ug)	0	0	0
Vitamin C (mg)	12.1	5.3	0.5
Cholesterol (mg)	0	0	0

While managing Chronic Kidney Disease (CKD) through a carefully monitored diet is crucial, it's only one piece of a larger, intricate puzzle. A balanced, low-sodium diet with controlled protein intake is essential, but it's not all-encompassing. A more holistic approach to CKD management exists, one that integrates not just dietary changes, but also lifestyle modifications.

Consider the impact of regular physical activity, adequate hydration, stress management, and quality sleep to overall wellbeing. How could these elements be intertwined with a CKD-friendly diet to create a comprehensive healthcare strategy? The answer lies in a broader perspective, one that values the interconnectedness of our daily habits. But what does this really mean for a patient with CKD? How does each aspect influence kidney health?

As we delve deeper into CKD management beyond dietary changes, you'll discover that there's more to this story than meets the eye...

Chapter 5:

Adapting Your Diet to Your Lifestyle

"**P**ersonalized nutrition is not just a trend, but a fundamental shift in how we approach health and wellness. Recognizing that each person has unique dietary needs is the cornerstone of effective nutritional therapy. It's about more than just the food on your plate; it's about how it interacts with your unique biochemistry."

Working with a Dietitian

I cannot stress enough and have repeatedly encouraged you and mentioned to you about "ask your dietitian this", "tell your dietitian about this", "let your dietitian confirm this" and so on.

At this point I don't think you need more convincing that a dietitian plays a crucial role in the management of Chronic Kidney Disease (CKD) and has the key responsibilities in your treatment process. But allow me to talk about some of these key roles so we can keep reminding ourselves how important they are for our overall wellness:

Nutritional Assessment

A dietitian conducts a comprehensive nutritional assessment to identify any nutritional deficiencies or excesses. They also evaluate a patient's dietary habits, preferences, and adherence to dietary recommendations.

Diet Planning

Based on the assessment, the dietitian creates an individualized diet plan. The dietitian takes into account the patient's CKD stage, other health conditions (like diabetes or hypertension), and dietary preferences.

Education

A dietitian educates the patient about the importance of nutrition in managing CKD. This includes explaining why certain foods should be limited (like those high in sodium, potassium, phosphorus) and others should be included.

Monitoring and Adjusting the Diet

The dietitian continually monitors the patient's health status, lab results, and adherence to the diet plan. They adjust the diet as necessary to account for changes in the patient's health.

Interdisciplinary Collaboration

The dietitian collaboratively works with the rest of the healthcare team, sharing their expertise on dietary issues to provide the best possible care for the patient.

Research and Advocacy

Dietitians stay informed about the latest research on CKD and nutrition. They also advocate for the nutritional needs of their patients.

Maximizing Your Dietician Appointments

With all those in mind, just like your doctors' visits, you may want to maximize your dietitian appointments which makes it crucial in managing Chronic Kidney Disease (CKD). Here are some strategies to make the most out of your time with your dietitian:

1. Preparation: Before your appointment, write down any questions or concerns you have. This could include queries about specific foods, how to manage your diet in social situations, or how to cope with dietary restrictions.

2. Honesty: Be honest with your dietitian about your eating habits, even if they're not always in line with dietary recommendations. Your dietitian is there to help, not judge. The more accurate information they have, the better they can tailor the dietary plan to your needs.

3. Open-Mindedness: Be open to trying new foods and recipes suggested by your dietitian. Diversifying your diet can make it more enjoyable and ensure you're getting a range of nutrients.

4. Record Keeping: Keep a food diary to track what and when you eat, as well as any symptoms you experience. This can provide valuable insights for your dietitian and may clarify areas where changes can be made.

5. Active Learning: Make an effort to understand the rationale behind dietary recommendations. This can help you make good dietary decisions in different situations.

6. Regular Feedback: Regularly communicate with your dietitian about what's working and what's not. This will help them adjust your diet plan as necessary.

7. Consistent Follow-Up: Regular appointments allow your dietitian to monitor your progress and make adjustments to your diet plan as needed. Don't skip these unless absolutely necessary.

8. Integration of Advice: Try to integrate the advice given by your dietitian into your daily life. This might require planning and prepping meals in advance or making conscious choices when dining out.

9. Involve Your Support System: If you're comfortable doing so, consider involving family members or close friends in your dietary management. They can provide support and help maintain the dietary changes you are making.

Remember, managing CKD is a team effort. Your dietitian is an important teammate in this journey, and maximizing your appointments with them can contribute significantly to your overall health and well-being. Finding one and being able to work consistently and openly would be one of the considerably major decisions and modifications you'll make in the course of your treatment plan.

Diet Adjustments for Common Comorbidities

Adjusting for Diabetes

Whether you have them or not, I would also like to take a little step further in including adjustments that you have to make for two of the most common chronic illnesses that may be due to or may have developed prior to CKD: Diabetes and Hypertension.

What's the relationship between Diabetes and Chronic Kidney Damage?

Diabetes is actually one of the risk factors and **leading cause to kidney failure.**

High blood glucose *(blood sugar)* can damage the blood vessels in your kidneys. When the blood vessels are damaged, your kidneys cannot clean your blood properly.

In turn, your body will retain more water and salt than it should, which can result in weight gain and ankle swelling.

Other health results include high blood pressure and having protein in your urine.

Since diabetes can damage the nerves in your body, it can cause a difficulty in emptying your bladder. With the pressure, it will result from your full bladder can back up and **injure the kidneys.**

What does that mean?

It means that if the urine stays in your bladder for a long period of time, you can develop an infection from the rapid growth of bacteria in urine that has a high sugar level.

So...what are the symptoms of diabetic kidney disease?

Most people with diabetic kidney disease *(diabetic nephropathy)* do not have symptoms because the only way to know if you have diabetic kidney disease is to **get your kidneys checked.** However, for some, there are early signs such as:

- Increased excretion of protein in urine
- Weight gain
- Leg or ankle swelling/cramps
- Increased need to urinate *(especially at night)*
- High blood pressure

Before we continue...I want to discuss the differences between diabetic kidney disease with type 1 & 2 diabetes.

Diabetic kidney disease is kidney damage that results from having diabetes. Because diabetes can cause high blood sugar, it can damage the part that filters the blood. For this reason, the damaged filter becomes leaky and then lets protein into your urine.

With *diabetic nephropathy*, it can progress to kidney failure compared to that of type 1 & 2 diabetes.

People with type 1 diabetes do not produce insulin, while type 2 diabetes do not respond to insulin. They both do not develop kidney disease that eventually progresses to kidney failure.

Now, moving on...

What lab tests do I need do to know that I have diabetic kidney disease?

First, take note of the signs or symptoms that you experienced since that will be the first thing that your doctor will ask you. Then, he or she will conduct a physical exam which afterwards, they will ask about your medical history. Once that's done, they will then refer you to a nephrologist or a diabetes specialist *(endocrinologist)*.

To really determine if you have diabetic kidney disease, you may be advised to do these tests and procedures:

- **Blood tests.** If you have diabetes, you will need blood tests to monitor your condition and determine how well your kidneys are working.
- **Urine tests.** Urine samples provide information about your kidney function and whether you have too much

protein in the urine. High levels of a protein called microalbumin may indicate your kidneys are being affected by the disease.

- **Imaging tests.** Your doctor may use X-rays and ultrasound to assess your kidneys' structure and size. You may also undergo CT scanning and magnetic resonance imaging (MRI) to determine how well blood is circulating within your kidneys. Other imaging tests may be used in some cases.

- **Renal function testing.** Your doctor can assess your kidneys' filtering capacity using renal analysis testing.

- **Kidney biopsy.** Your doctor may recommend a kidney biopsy to remove a sample of kidney tissue. You'll be given a numbing medication (local anesthetic). Then your doctor will use a thin needle to remove small pieces of kidney tissue for examination under a microscope.

Okay….how about medication?

In the early stages of the disease, your treatment plan may include various medications that will help:

- **Control high blood pressure.** Medications called angiotensin-converting enzyme (ACE) inhibitors and angiotensin II receptor blockers (ARBs) are used to treat high blood pressure. Using both of these together isn't advised because of increased side effects. Studies support the goal of a blood pressure reading below 140/90 millimeters of mercury (mm Hg) depending on your age and overall risk of cardiovascular disease.

- **Manage high blood sugar.** Several medications have been shown to help control high blood sugar in people with diabetic nephropathy. Studies support the goal of an average hemoglobin A1C of less than 7%.

- **Lower high cholesterol.** Cholesterol-lowering drugs called statins are used to treat high cholesterol and reduce protein in the urine.
- **Foster bone health.** Medications that help manage your calcium phosphate balance are important in maintaining healthy bones.
- **Control protein in urine.** Medications can often reduce the level of the protein albumin in the urine and improve kidney function.

Along the way, your doctor may recommend follow-up testing at regular intervals to see whether your kidney disease remains stable or progresses.

Can diabetic kidney disease be treated?

Treatment for diabetic kidney disease include:

- Controlling and managing blood sugar levels
- Controlling high blood pressure
- Reducing dietary protein intake
- Avoiding medications that may damage kidneys
- Treat urinary tract infections
- Exercise/Lose weight *(under the supervision of a physician)*

If I have diabetic kidney disease and CKD, how should I balance both diets?

It's true that the **right diet** helps your body function properly. However, figuring out what to eat especially if you have both diabetes and Chronic Kidney Disease can be a major challenge because when one meal plan may be good for you, it may not be good for the other. Which is why, **you need to consult a registered nutritionist dietitian** who is trained in both diabetes and Chronic Kidney Disease nutrition for this one. Together you will create a diet plan that will help keep your blood sugar levels steady and reduce the waste and fluid your kidneys have to handle. He or she will give nutritional guidelines to you on how much nutrients *(SPPP)* you can have each day and limit or avoid them while planning your meals.

Remember that portion is also important to do. If you remember from our previous lesson, I taught you how to do so below:

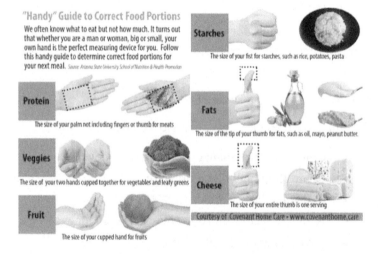

"Handy" Guide to Correct Food Portions

We often know what to eat but not how much. It turns out that whether you are a man or woman, big or small, your own hand is the perfect measuring device for you. Follow this handy guide to determine correct food portions for your next meal. *Source: Arizona State University School of Nutrition & Health Promotion*

Protein — The size of your palm not including fingers or thumb for meats

Veggies — The size of your two hands cupped together for vegetables and leafy greens

Fruit — The size of your cupped hand for fruits

Starches — The size of your fist for starches, such as rice, potatoes, pasta

Fats — The size of the tip of your thumb for fats, such as oil, mayo, peanut butter.

Cheese — The size of your entire thumb is one serving

Courtesy of Covenant Home Care • www.covenanthome.care

But if you want, you could talk to your nutritionist regarding tips to accurately measure a serving size because what may be measured as one serving size on a regular diet may count as three times more on a kidney diet.

The meal planning also includes eating meals and snacks that have the same size and calorie/carbohydrate content at certain times of the day in order to keep your blood glucose at an even level. Again, it's important to check your blood glucose levels often and share the results with your doctor.

Believe it or not, diabetes and Chronic Kidney Disease share a lot of the same food BUT of course, there are some important differences.

So, what can I eat then?

What I will list down below are examples of food choices that are usually recommended on a typical renal diabetic diet since this list will be based on sodium, potassium, phosphorus, protein, and high sugar content of foods.

CARBOHYDRATE FOODS

Milk and non dairy products

- Skim/Fat-free milk
- Non-dairy creamer
- Sugar-free yogurt
- Sugar-free ice cream
- Sugar-free non dairy frozen desserts

BREADS AND STARCHES

- Whole wheat
- Whole grain
- Unsalted crackers
- White/Whole Wheat Pasta
- Grits

FRUITS AND JUICES

- Apples/Applesauce/apple juice
- Raspberries
- Blueberries

- Low-sugar cranberry juice
- Grape/grape juice
- Grapefruit

STARCHY VEGETABLES

- Corn
- Peas
- Potatoes *(soaked in order to reduce potassium)*

NON-STARCHY VEGETABLES

- Asparagus
- Beets
- Broccoli
- Brussels sprouts
- Cauliflower
- Cabbage
- Cucumber

HIGH-PROTEIN FOODS (Meats, cheeses, and eggs

- Lean cuts of meat
- Eggs
- Poultry
- Low-cholesterol egg substitute

HIGHER-FAT FOODS (Seasonings and calories)

- Sour cream
- Low-fat mayonnaise
- Low-fat cream cheese

Again, these are all just recommendations on a typical renal diabetic diet. You need to ask your nutritionist if you can have any of these listed foods and make sure that you ask your recommended servings size as well. I want to share four (4) tips on how to keep your kidneys healthy with diabetic kidney disease.

The best way to slow it down or prevent it from progressing is to try to reach your blood glucose and blood pressure goals. Healthy lifestyle habits and taking in your prescribed medications can help you achieve those goals and at the same time, improve your overall health.

1. Reach your blood glucose goals

A healthcare professional will need to test your A1C. This is a blood test that will show your average blood glucose level over the past three months, which is different from the blood glucose checks that you may do yourself at home.

The higher your A1C number, the higher your blood glucose levels have been during the past three months. The goal for many people with diabetes is **below 7 percent.** However, you may ask your health care team what your goal should be since reaching it will help protect your kidneys. After which, you will use those results to discuss with your healthcare team that will help decide on food, physical activity, and medicines.

One more thing to ask your healthcare team is how often you should check your blood glucose level.

2. Control and manage your blood pressure

High blood pressure *(hypertension)* happens when the pressure of your blood against the walls of your blood vessels increases. If left uncontrolled, it could cause stroke, heart attack, and Chronic Kidney Disease.

For this reason, ask your health care team to help you set and reach your blood pressure goal. The blood pressure goal for most people with diabetes is below 140/90mmHg.

Taking in prescribed medication that can help lower blood pressure and slow down kidney damage is also important.

3. Develop or maintain healthy lifestyle habits

Forming healthy lifestyle habits can help you reach your blood glucose and blood pressure goals. Following these steps below will help you keep your kidneys healthy:

- Stop smoking
- Work with a nutritionist dietitian to develop a diabetes meal plan and limit salt and sodium
- Get physical! Make it part of your routine *(with the supervision of a physician)*
- Stay at or get to a healthy weight
- Get enough sleep. Be sure to aim for 7-8 hours of sleep each night.

4. Take prescribed medications

Taking in medications may be an important part of your treatment plan as your health care professional will prescribe them based on your specific needs and can help meet your blood glucose and blood pressure goals.

High Blood Pressure and CKD

I know it's been briefly discussed almost althroughout this book and even when talking about diabetic nephropathy, but I want us to take a closer look at high blood pressure's (hypertension) relationship with Chronic Kidney Disease, the negative effects of high blood pressure, and how to manage it.

So, are you ready? If you are, let's start with what it means...

Blood pressure refers to the force of blood against the walls of your blood vessels as your heart pumps blood around your body. If it becomes too high, you can be diagnosed with high blood pressure or hypertension. Simply put, it's the pressure that prevails in the blood vessels.

Did you know that your blood pressure results are written with two values?

- The upper pressure *(systolic pressure)* is the pressure you have at the moment your heart contracts and pushes the blood through all blood vessels.
- The bottom number *(diastolic pressure)* indicates the pressure you have when your heart relaxes between the contractions. The heart functions as a pump.

Normal Blood Pressure

It is important for everyone to maintain normal blood pressure, appropriate to age, especially for patients with CKD.

Your blood pressure should be lower than 130/80 mmHg. If it's higher than 130/80 mmHg, it puts extra strain on your heart and blood vessels. This increases your risk of developing cardiovascular disease. The blood vessels can get thicker walls, the heart is negatively affected, just like the eyes. In short, the higher the blood pressure over a longer period of time, the greater the risk of a heart attack, or stroke.

High blood pressure is one of the causes of CKD, making it more serious. But, it also works the other way around. CKD sooner or later causes blood pressure to rise. This is partly because the kidneys can no longer properly regulate blood pressure. In other words: High blood pressure and CKD reinforce each other in a negative way. So, how can you determine if your blood pressure is too high?

The only way is to measure it with a blood pressure monitoring device. To make things worse, high blood pressure may not reveal obvious symptoms. That's why it has been called a "silent killer". A single reading of high blood pressure doesn't confirm that you have it. It is confirmed through follow-up visits to your doctor or clinic. Symptoms of severely elevated blood pressure include:

- Headache
- Confusion
- Blurry or double vision
- Bloody (pink colored) urine
- Nose bleed

When visiting your doctor, make sure to have your blood pressure measured. During this visit, they may focus on lowering and managing your blood pressure – one of the most important goals of treatment to improve and maintain your kidney functions.

Treatment Plan

Well, a treatment plan is necessary especially when it should be based on your CKD stage. In some cases, your doctor may recommend you to see a specialist in high blood pressure or CKD. The goals of the treatment are:

- To lower your blood pressure,
- To keep kidney disease from getting worse, and
- To lower your chances of getting heart disease.

116

To help reach these goals, you will need a combination of lifestyle changes, such as switching to a kidney-healthy diet, exercise, and taking medications especially prescribed for your condition.

To Do's to Lower Your Blood Pressure

But for now, we would like to focus more on the first goal which is to lower your blood pressure because it can have a positive ripple effect. Here are 6 ways you can do that:

☑ To Do 1: Exercise

- Exercise is important for heart health.
- Set a goal to exercise for 30 minutes a day, 5 days per week.
- Try walking or dancing.

☑ To Do 2: Maintain a healthy weight

Being overweight normally increases blood pressure, while reduced weight can lower blood pressure.

☑ To Do 3: Quit smoking

Nicotine causes the smallest blood vessels to constrict and thereby increases blood pressure.

☑ To Do 4: Limit sodium intake

Stop adding salt to your meals. Try to prepare the meal with as little salt as possible. Salt ensures that you retain moisture and that again causes the blood pressure to rise. If you use less salt you will quickly get used to the taste and feel better.

☑ To Do 5: Take prescribed medications

It is very important that you take the blood pressure medication that the doctor prescribed and that you do exactly as he has advised. You can get one or two different blood pressure medications prescribed which all have a slightly different effect and together ensure that your high blood pressure will decrease.

☑ To Do 6: Reduce stress

Stress is normal. And yes, stress can be detrimental, but ONLY IF YOU LET IT. Properly dealing with stress not only helps you manage it, but it will also serve to strengthen you and make you more resilient.

Constant and excessive stress does take a toll on your health. This is why stress management is very important, especially for people with a chronic kidney condition.

So, how does stress affect the kidneys? Usually, the body's response to stress and anxiety are the following:

- Increase in breathing and heart rate
- Blood pressure spikes
- Pupil dilation
- Muscle tension
- Increase in fat and sugar levels in the blood

These responses are normal and can actually help you when dealing with crises and immediate danger.

However, constantly experiencing these bodily reactions because of high stress levels for long periods takes a toll on your health.

I hope that I was able to shed light, or add important bits of information in the management of comorbidities that may have come along with CKD, or help you prevent them from sabotaging your goals for health. Now that that's out of the way, how about we take care of other serious business? Like planning your lunch out next weekend?

"Am I even allowed to do that?"...

Sure you are, and I might have just the thing to help you out!

Chapter 6:

Handling Special Occasions and Dining Out

*I*n the heart of Foodville lived a kidney patient, Kevin, with a mighty appetite. Dining out was his hobby, but health was his priority.

When "Salty Spud" opened, renowned for its potato delights, Kevin's face lit up. However, he knew the drill: no excess salt, no potassium overload.

As the waiter recommended the "Spud Supreme," Kevin's mouth watered. But he ordered the "Low-Sodium Salad" instead. The waiter blinked, surprised. "Are you sure, sir? It's rather...bland."

"Absolutely," replied Kevin, with a twinkle in his eye.

The salad arrived, plain as plain can be. Then, Kevin unveiled his secret weapon - a small bottle of homemade, kidney-friendly seasoning. A sprinkle here, a dash there, and the salad was transformed!

That night, Kevin left the restaurant, belly full, spirits high. Health restrictions couldn't dampen his dining adventures. Kevin, the ever-ready foodie, had once again found joy in the culinary battlefield.

Navigating Different Eating Situations

That was a little too playful, wasn't it? But let me ask you, have you ever been tempted to break your diet when you're eating at home or at a restaurant? Well, the reality is, **we've all been there.**

Whether it is with friends or with family, it can be quite stressful to stay on-track with your needs to make healthy choices and be mindful of what you are eating, especially if they're not going through the same journey as you. This anxiety can lead to poor food decisions and hinder you from achieving a healthier lifestyle. Growing up, our parents are our first role models and teachers, so we tend to mirror our behavior after what we have been shown or taught. If we have always experienced an unhealthy lifestyle, we are more likely to make poor dietary choices — even as an adult.

Therefore, it can be difficult to overcome that kind of eating style, especially if we are dining with our family or friends. Such situations can be a trigger and may push us back into our old eating habits.

Dining out with friends can be just as stressful because you are not conforming to the "norm" of the social circle. Most of us, *I know I do*, want to feel included, so we tend to give into "peer pressure" especially in a social setting that involves eating. Most of the time, this leads to guilt or shame because you abandoned everything that you have been working hard for.

However, in making small changes in our thoughts and behaviors, we can better handle some of the situations mentioned above that can help keep us on track and positively impact those we care about. Every step that you take to improve your overall health and well-being is a positive step in **the right direction.**

Eating alone at home

When you are at home you can of course think about what you will eat. You can plan food so that it contains exactly the amount of protein you are allowed to have. Certainly if you cook yourself. Do not add salt to the food.

Eating with family at home

When more people in the family eat together, things get a bit more complicated. Not everyone in the family will appreciate the protein-restricted meals. There are at least two ways to work around this problem:

- One way is to prepare different dishes; for those who have chronic kidney damage and for the rest of the family. For example: for the kidney patient, instead a bowl of yogurt or custard for dessert or no cheese sauce over the vegetables. And vegetables, potatoes and meat without salt for the kidney patient and with salt for the rest of the family.
- The other way is that you prepare food that most of the family likes without thinking about the kidney patient. Then it is up to you to determine what you eat or not eat (or less) of. For example: you take more potatoes, more vegetables and less meat (and preferably an extra cube of diet-margarine through the food). Do not add salt to the food. The family members can add salt to their own dish if necessary.

In most families, it will be some sort of mix of these two ways. Sometimes you can prepare something for the kidney patient.

But usually everyone eats the same and the difference is in the quantities. Of course, you are the one having CKD and therefore you should be able to assess what you can and cannot eat. You are the one in control of the grams of protein you eat.

Eating at work

When you bring your food from home to work, you decide what you eat - food and drinks appropriate for someone with CKD. If you eat in the staff restaurant it would be nice if you can choose different dishes. Again, as a kidney patient you must have enough knowledge to make a responsible choice - for instance, choose something of which you roughly know how much protein it contains, and of which you can take the right amounts.

Dining out

The best thing is of course if you can choose your restaurant yourself. For someone with chronic kidney disease, a "steakhouse" where mainly large steaks are served is not the best option. It is best to go to a restaurant with a wide and varied range of dishes, where you have more "kidney-friendly" dishes. Ask if they can prepare the food without any added salt.

The important thing is that you have so much knowledge of the amount of protein in the various

foods that you know which dishes to avoid, of which you can take bits and from which you can take somewhat larger portions. You can have that knowledge by plunging into the tables a little further in the book.

*For Chef Duane, one of his **AHA! Moments** where he felt normal again was when he ordered side dishes at a Mexican restaurant and felt normal. Not only that, he could also eat rice, beans, guacamole with "no salt added" chips, and learned to* *make spinach and mushroom enchiladas. Because of this, he doesn't miss the beef tacos or the chicken taquitos.*

If you're trying to limit animal protein like him, here's his advice: **Read the entire menu.** *Read it like it's a grocery list. Yes, a grocery list. But you have to look at the side dishes with every entree on the menu.*

What he does is he'd take all the side dishes and request a plate be made into a meal. But he cautions you that with this kind of creativity, it can cause some surprises when the bill comes at the end of the meal.

Eat with family or friends

All good hosts and hostesses ask themselves: what can I prepare for a person with chronic kidney disease, what can he have? That is quite thoughtful and nice.

An answer to the question can be: "In principle I eat everything, so prepare something you want". And then you adjust how much you eat, that is, a little bit of what contains a lot of protein and more of other things. But ask if they don't add salt to it.

Another answer can of course be that you indicate more precisely what you like and that you explain something about the protein-restricted diet and about cooking without salt. Most people who invite someone with chronic kidney damage would like to make an effort to offer something suitable, that is after all the reason they ask.

The most important thing is that you stick to the number of grams of protein per day that are recommended. So if you take a little more protein with lunch then you need one take a little less when eating at night - and vice versa. It is about the average dividend amount per day. And all this of course with the note that you are well.

Eat if you go by plane

Eating on board of a plane can become a minor problem, as there usually is little to choose. You usually have to take what is there and then you have to determine what and how much you can eat from what is available.

Another way is to prepare, for example, a vegetarian and sodium meal that is likely to have less protein (and no salt) than the normal meat and fish dishes. Watch out for soy dishes, which are high in protein. With some airlines you can even eat protein-restricted and sodium-restricted foods, if you order this well in advance.

Strategies on Staying On-Track

When the time comes where you will feel pressured to eat something that you shouldn't, here are **four (4) tips to help yourself stay in control and on track with your health:**

1. Visualize yourself making good choices

Scientific research shows that if you visualize yourself doing something that has a successful outcome, you are able to reinforce the neural pathways in your brain and **increase your chances for success**.

For example, if you're afraid to go to a party because you know the host will expect you to eat the meals they have prepared, visualize yourself enjoying the party, and calmly explaining to the host that you're practicing health-consciousness.

Imagine yourself feeling calm, relaxed, happy, and satisfied. You'll notice that when you mentally prepare yourself in this manner beforehand, you'll experience much more success at being able to avoid certain foods.

2. Eat a healthy meal beforehand

If you're getting ready to attend an event that you know will offer unhealthy foods, make plans to eat before you go so you won't be hungry, tempted, or forced to eat anything at the event.

For example, eat a large green salad followed by a chicken breast and some steamed veggies to give yourself the nourishment and energy you need to sustain yourself throughout the course of the event.

These types of foods will also provide you with a lasting feeling of fullness that will help prevent you from being hungry and experiencing cravings later on.

3. Bring your own healthy dish

If you're attending a party or event where bringing food is allowed, make your own healthy meals or side dishes at home and bring them with you to the party.

In most cases, the host will be thankful that you contributed to the party. Bring homemade salad and dressing, or crackers made with healthy ingredients and hummus dip.

4. Assess your options before digging in

If the event you're attending is offering catered food, or food laid out in buffet style, take a moment to walk through and assess your options before loading up your plate.

Look for salads, vegetables, drumsticks, and other whole foods that aren't processed or made with artificial ingredients. Start off with a large plate of salad, then go back for various other whole foods that won't harm your kidneys.

As far as drinks go, stick to water and avoid drinking sugary fruit juice or punch. If alcohol is being served, limit yourself to one or two glasses of wine or consume small amounts of liquor without adding mixers. This too will depend on your healthcare team's advice on alcohol consumption. If you are unsure, let's stick with water!

And that's it! As mentioned, taking the first step is the most difficult to make. But once you take it, everything will fall into place.

You will become more invested in your journey to a healthier lifestyle. Who knows, along the way, you may even inspire those around you to eat healthier. You will feel better about yourself and the choices that you are making.

Every step in the right direction will get you one step closer to achieving your goals of creating the healthy lifestyle you desire.

While social pressure can be quite stressful, **it can be managed.** Remember that **YOU ARE IN CONTROL.** Just don't forget to take the first step because your body and mind will thank you in the future.

Chapter 7:
Exercise and CKD Management

*A*s Dr. Patel explained the importance of exercise in managing Chronic Kidney Disease, Alex felt a pang of guilt. Those unused running shoes gathered dust in the corner, a stark reminder of abandoned resolutions. "Start slow, Alex," Dr. Patel advised, "your kidneys will thank you." The next morning, lacing up those shoes, Alex stepped outside, heart pounding. Nervous energy filled the air. The jog was tougher than expected, but it had begun. Just as Alex was finding rhythm, a sharp pain shot through his side. Doubled over, he saw a figure approach. "Are you okay?" the stranger asked.

Alex grimaced, clutching his side. His breaths becoming short and fast. "Just...a cramp," he panted, trying to wave the stranger away. But the stranger, a woman with kind eyes and a runner's physique, didn't budge.

"Try slow, deep breaths," she suggested, her tone laced with concern. Alex followed her advice, the pain slowly subsiding. As he straightened up, he noticed her runner's bib. 'Marathoner', it read.

"You new to running?" she asked, handing him a water bottle. Alex nodded, explaining about his CKD and the doctor's advice. A smile of understanding crossed her face. "It's tough at first,

but it gets better," she said, "Want some company on your journey?"

How about you? Yes, you! Do you want some company in this journey?

While I can't technically be physically with you, let me help you with the following:

- Understand the role of exercise in improving your kidney health,
- Learn how to sketch out your own exercise plan and overcome common objections and excuses,
- Learn exercise tips and tricks that you can follow and take inspiration from, and
- Learn how to combine both diet and exercise.

Before we begin, I'd like to share this piece of advice with you:

"How we spend our days is, of course, how we spend our lives." - Annie Dillard

Now, it may seem like we're stating the obvious. But the truth is, not everyone grasps the gravity of those words.

Few of us are consciously aware that everything we do—down to the tiniest, most seemingly inconsequential action—defines the quality of the life we live. But what does that have to do with today's discussion? Or with your kidneys for that matter?

Well, we brought it up because today, we're going to talk about a particular action that a lot of people with kidney conditions have questions about: **exercise!**

Normally, exercise is a vital part of a healthy daily routine. But considering you have CKD, you might be wondering what effect working out will have on your kidneys and your life. *Should you*

still do it, or should you take it easy because of your condition?
If you're not sure of the answer, worry not; that's the first
question we'll answer today.

A few years back, the answer would have been a resounding
"no".

Doctors used to think that kidney disease patients shouldn't
exercise—vigorous physical activity was too much for them to
handle and would do more harm than good. But things have
changed a lot since then. Now we know different things. The
newest research shows that:

> ### Kidney disease patients who exercise
> ### enjoy a lot of health benefits.

However, there is a **bit of a catch.** As someone with a kidney
condition, your exercise routine should be tailored to fit your
condition. We'll talk about how you can do that later on. For
now, let's go into more detail on those "health benefits" we just
mentioned.

The Benefits of Exercise

Here's a list of the major advantages you can get by engaging in
proper exercise:

1. Lower blood pressure

This can have a direct effect on your renal health, since high
blood pressure is one of those conditions that **can cause kidney
function to decline**. Keeping it in check is crucial.

2. Reduced risk of diabetes or better glucose control

Diabetes is another condition that has a direct effect on kidney
function. If you don't have it, do everything in your power to

keep it that way. If you already have diabetes, exercise is still beneficial, since it helps your body control your glucose level better.

3. Improved muscle strength and function

Weakness and fatigue is a common complaint for those with kidney conditions. Exercise can alleviate that by developing your muscles which leaves you feeling stronger and more able to move around.

4. Helps you lose excess weight or maintain your current weight

Being overweight really isn't a problem you want to have on top of dealing with kidney disease—you'll be at risk of developing even more health complications. A healthy weight is vital.

5. Lower levels of blood fats (like triglycerides and cholesterol)

At high levels, triglycerides and cholesterol can damage your blood vessels. Kidney function depends a lot on the condition of your kidneys' blood vessels, so make sure to keep them damage-free.

6. Better sleep

Few things are as relaxing as a good night's sleep, right? Sleep is when our bodies rest and regenerate, and studies show that catching enough Z's can do wonders for your health.

7. Reduces anxiety and depression

Your emotions and outlook can have a surprisingly large impact on your physical condition. Exercising encourages the release of "*happy hormones*", combating depression, or simply giving your mood a lift.

And there you have it! Those are some great benefits, right? All that through the simple act of proper exercise.h

But before you start working out, there are some things you should take into consideration, especially because you have a kidney condition… To find out what those are, read on!

Personalizing Your Exercise Plan

You'll notice that I mentioned the words *"proper exercise"* more than once.

The reason for that is because we want to emphasize the importance not just of exercising, but of **exercising the right way.**

And that means personalizing your workout — taking into account your strengths and weaknesses, as well as any health conditions that may hinder you. But planning the right exercise program can be a bit tricky, so it's best to have the opinion of a health professional who is familiar with your condition.

Together, you can decide on the specifics, like:

- **Type:** What type of exercise should you do?
- **Frequency:** How often should you do it?
- **Duration:** How long should you do it each time?
- **Intensity:** How hard should you push yourself?

Those are basic questions you need to answer before you begin any exercise plan. Personalize your exercise plan by choosing the right type, frequency, duration, and intensity of exercise.

Too Busy **For Exercise?**

Sometimes, it doesn't matter whether there's an exercise plan in place or not, because we often get in our own way when it's time to work out.

You can come up with a thousand reasons why you're "too busy" to exercise right now, but here's the truth:

You should never be too busy to prioritize your own health.

Putting your health first sounds like common sense, but unfortunately, it's not something that comes easy for many of us.

So to help you put all your objections behind, here's the University of Houston's list of the most common excuses we make to avoid exercise, and counterpoints for each of them:

EXCUSE	COUNTERPOINT
"I'm too busy, I only have 20 minutes"	Not only is that enough time, **it's far better than doing nothing**.
"I'm too tired"	Exercise will give you energy. You'll feel better when you're done.
"My husband or wife won't join me"	**Set a good example** that may inspire your partner to join you.
"I'm on vacation"	What better time to exercise than when you have so much free time? Walking is a great travel pastime.

"I can come up with more reasons **not to exercise"**	That still doesn't mean you can't.

We hope that with the examples in this list, you can identify the excuses you use to avoid exercising and come up with your own counterpoints.

Exercise doesn't have to be boring. Tying it into your hobbies, like dancing or hiking, can make it a bit easier to deal with. Even chores, like walking the dog or tending the garden, can be considered exercise as well.

Which is why we'll be showing you some actual exercise routines through easy-to-follow videos. But before I do, here's what Lee Haney, a fitness expert and champion bodybuilder once said:

*"Exercise to **stimulate** not to **annihilate**; The world wasn't formed in a day and neither were we. **Set small gals and build upon them**." – Lee Haney*

Don't exercise with the goal of eliminating your health issues as quickly as possible, because honestly, **nothing will change overnight. Be patient with yourself.** Remember to set goals that are **achievable and realistic**. Work on achieving those goals, one step at a time, and eventually, you'll notice a big change!

Types of Exercises That Should Be In Your Plan

Since we talked about the four aspects of exercise: *type, frequency, duration, and intensity,* we'll focus on the **type** first. There are three major types of exercise that should always be part of any workout plan:

1. Flexibility Exercises

Stretching activities fall under this category. They're usually used as warm-ups for exercise routines. Here are some sample routines: *(scan the code with your phone camera to watch the exercise videos)*

- **Desk Stretches** - A series of flexibility exercises you can perform anytime, even on your desk. *(https://youtu.be/DKnJh2wJvHE)*

- **Hamstring Stretch -** A stretch you can do with a simple tool, like a belt. *(https://youtu.be/2-plTieJyFs)*

2. Aerobic Exercises

Aerobic exercises improve your endurance. It involves moving large muscle groups in a continuous way. These are also used as **warm up and cooling down exercises** when done lightly for a short period. But when done for longer and with a higher intensity, they can be the main focus of your exercise routine.

Good examples include **walking, running, swimming, dancing, and cycling**—whether outdoors, or indoors on a stationary bike, as you will see in the next slide. Here are some sample routines:

- **Seated Bike** - A good example of aerobic exercise which requires equipment. You can also use a regular bike instead and go outdoors.
  (https://youtu.be/X7NYGzDMzYo)

- **High Knees** - One of many aerobic exercises you can do that are easy and don't require equipment.
  (https://youtu.be/SC_Y1Ri_S6I)

- **Jumping Jacks** *(optional)* - A familiar exercise that can be a warm up when done in a short period, but can also be high intensity when done longer.
  (https://youtu.be/CV_BOYUA63c)

3. Resistance Exercises

The focus of this type of exercise is to improve your strength. That's why they are also called **strength training exercises.** They are typically the main part of routines, which means they are done **after warming up and before cooling down.**

Examples include weight lifting, and activities that involve lifting your own weight like **jumps**, **squats, lifts, lunges, push-ups (and its modified forms), and even climbing stairs.**

Important Note: Overall, resistance exercises are beneficial, but since you have a kidney condition, avoid routines that require heavy lifting. If you want to push yourself harder, do more repetitions instead of using heavier weights. Here's another set of sample routines:

- Forward Stepping Lunge - A resistance exercise you can do with or without additional weights. *(https://youtu.be/LuqNTCGIqU0)*
- Bicep Curl - A very simple weightlifting exercise. You can gradually increase the difficulty level by doing more repetitions. *(https://youtu.be/S-jAVi4NFVs)*

Duration, Frequency, and Intensity: Tips and Tricks

Now that we're done with the types of exercise, let's talk about the other three aspects: duration, frequency, and intensity.

Let's go through them one at a time:

1. Frequency. This refers to how often you should exercise. As you might expect, this varies from case to case, but generally, most people should exercise **at least 3 days a week.** Quick Tips:

- **Do not exercise on consecutive days.** Leave a "rest day" in between your workout sessions. This prevents muscle damage and fatigue.
- **Alternate between aerobic and resistance exercises for the main parts of your routines.** Different types of exercise have different effects on your body, so make sure to strike a balance between the two for maximum benefit.

2. Duration. This refers to how long your exercises should be. Ideally, you should aim for at least 30 minutes for each session.

- **Don't worry if you think 30 minutes is too long for you.** For now, just go with the duration you're most comfortable with and gradually increase the time until you reach 30 minutes. For example, you can start at 15 minutes, and then increase each session 1 minute at a time.

- **Spend around 5-10 minutes on warming up.** Do this so that your body isn't "shocked" by sudden activity. You can start with light aerobic exercise, and then move on to stretching.

- **Cool down before stopping.** Gradually end each session with exercises that are similar to your warm up. Stopping your routine all of a sudden (without a cool down) can cause negative effects, like dizziness or nausea.

3. Intensity. This refers to how hard you should push yourself while exercising.

We've told you before that exercise should be personalized, and this is especially important when determining the intensity of your workout. Here are some quick tips to check for the right intensity:

- **Your breathing shouldn't be so hard that you can't talk while exercising.** You can check this by talking to yourself (or someone else if possible) once in a while during your workout.

- **You should feel completely normal an hour after ending your session.** If you don't, you're probably pushing yourself too hard. Slow down and cut back on the number of exercises or repetitions you're doing.

- **Your muscles shouldn't be sore enough that you can't exercise for the next session.** Consistency is important. Don't set a pace you can't keep up with.

- **Aim for a comfortable push.** Exerting yourself is part of working out, so you should feel like you're pushing yourself – just not too much.

Remember, starting slowly and progressing gradually over time is the best way to exercise.

Don't forget Mr. Lee Haney's quote at the beginning of this chapter – exercises to stimulate, not to annihilate. Give your body enough time to adapt to your increasing physical activity.

Making Sense of the Whole Package: Integrating Nutrition, Diet and Exercise

Diet and exercise go hand in hand. If your goal is to achieve better overall health—and that includes your kidney health, of course—then you can't have one without the other.

Both are also vital for weight management. This is especially important, since for someone with a kidney condition, any problems with weight (or fat) will likely have more consequences down the line…

To sum it up simply, it's like this:

Diet controls weight, while exercise controls body composition.

Basically, **what you eat** determines how fast you lose or gain weight, and **physical activity** determines if you're losing or gaining fat or muscle. I know that might be just a bit confusing, so let me clarify with a few examples:

1. If you want to lose weight...

Losing weight depends mainly on your diet. If you're eating too many calories, you won't lose weight no matter how much exercise you put in.

On the flip side, if you eat too little calories, you're starving yourself. Your body responds to that by trying to save as much energy as possible, which means less weight loss for you. **Aim for a daily calorie intake that's around 300-500 calories below your daily recommendation.** This is just enough to prevent your body from going into *"starvation mode"*.

Exercise contributes by controlling your body composition as your weight goes down. **If you don't exercise, your body will burn off muscle instead of fat during weight loss.** This will leave you feeling weak and fatigued.

But when you do exercise, you keep (or maybe increase) your muscle mass while dropping off the pounds in fat. This is the healthy type of weight loss that you should aim for—it should leave you feeling stronger and more energetic, and not the other way around.

2. If you want to maintain your weight (and lose fat while gaining muscle)...

If you're currently at your ideal weight—and want it to stay that way—then your focus should be on exercise. Still, you shouldn't disregard your diet altogether.

A healthy balanced diet is vital for keeping up your energy level, repairing and replenishing your muscles, and promoting the growth of new muscle.

3. If you want to gain weight (by adding muscle, not fat)…

You have to eat more!

Of course, it goes without saying you should eat healthy food—trying to gain weight is not an excuse to eat anything you want. To gain weight the healthy way, a balanced diet is vital. You just need to increase your portion sizes.

Trying to gain weight is also not an excuse to slack in the exercise department.

You want to add muscle mass to your body, not fat, so exercise is an absolute must. Just make sure that your diet makes up for the calories you burn during exercise.

Your Diet and Activity Plan

**"A goal without a plan is just a wish." -
Antoine de Saint-Exupery**

In order for a goal to become reality, you need a plan to make it happen!

Right now, your goal is to maintain your kidney health. To do that, you need a diet and activity plan. It doesn't have to be ultra-detailed, just clear enough to help you stay on track and not lose focus.

To get started, here are a few questions you should be able to answer:

1. What are your bad health habits? What nutrients should you be limiting? (For example, sodium or phosphorus, maybe?)
2. How many calories do you consume per day? Is it more than what you need, less, or just enough?
3. How much exercise do you get right now? Is it enough?

4. What healthy foods and recipes do you like? What physical activities do you enjoy?

5. What challenges and roadblocks have you encountered in the past?

You can use your answers to those questions to come up with a diet and exercise plan that addresses your personal needs.

The first three of those questions are all about self-assessment. Before you can come up with a plan, you need to get a good idea of where you are at the moment—and where you want to be.

The 4th question is the key to creating a plan that's enjoyable for you—or at least, one that won't make you miserable! Use the answers you have to create a plan that's tailored to your preferences.

The last question identifies the things that have stopped you from being healthy in the past, so you can avoid them in the present. Don't make the same mistakes twice!

You have all you need to create a great diet and exercise plan... and you're good to go!

Chapter 8:
Stress, Mental Health, and CKD

The mental health aspect of managing Chronic Kidney Disease (CKD) is frequently overlooked, yet it is a crucial component of comprehensive patient care. Living with CKD is not just a physical challenge; it is an emotional and psychological battle as well. The diagnosis often brings a profound life change, triggering feelings of fear, stress, and uncertainty.

Additionally, the ongoing management of the disease - the strict dietary restrictions, the regular medical appointments, and the necessary lifestyle alterations - can cause significant psychological distress. It is paramount that healthcare providers recognize this and integrate mental health care into the treatment plans. Psychological support, including counselling and therapy, should be readily available to patients, helping them navigate their feelings and cope more effectively with their condition. The interplay between physical health and mental well-being is undeniable; addressing both is key for improving the overall quality of life for CKD patients.

Understanding the Mental Impact of CKD

A 2019 study on neuropharmacology states that "neuropsychiatric conditions including depression, anxiety disorders, and cognitive impairment are prevalent in patients with chronic kidney disease (CKD)". And often, these conditions can further prevent patients' progress.

Because of such, it's crucial for us to learn about the role of your mental health too. This includes your thoughts, feelings, and behaviors related to improving your condition.

So remember: don't stick to your health's physical aspect alone. Your health care team can provide you with all the information about your condition and even hand you over all the medications you need to improve your health.

However, being a mere recipient of your health care is sometimes not enough. You should play an active role in your own health. Because if you lacked the will to improve or recover, what use are all the medicines in the world?

Now think about our physical and mental structures having their own natural 'defense mechanisms', a 'first line of defense', or 'guards and protectors'. A simple example would be our skin as it acts as a protective barrier between invaders (pathogens) and our bodies.

Our 'psyche' (our mind) is also protected from things that prevent us from fully realizing our wills or motivations. But sometimes, our mental health isn't strong enough to combat these struggles which can make us unable to cope up with our condition properly.

And this is why we're here to talk about how you can strengthen your mental health: so that you can confront and break down the barriers that impede your recovery and improvement.

In the very beginning of this book, we talked about the different goal setting barriers you face when adjusting your diet. To overcome them, we laid down a few examples of SMART (Specific, Measurable, Action-Oriented, Realistic, and Time-framed) goals and encouraged you to use it in every goal you set.

Now, we will tackle another barrier related to healthy eating that is common among CKD patients---your motivational barriers relevant to your attitude and beliefs.

Motivational Barriers and How to Overcome Them

A qualitative study conducted in 2019 lists 4 barriers that interfere with people's motivation to improve their diet or accustom themselves to healthy eating. we've renamed them to "Bogus Barriers" because they're exactly that - untrue.

☹ *Bogus Barrier 1: "Eating healthy food is undesirable"*

Some people often consider healthy eating as undesirable because they have a general perception that healthy foods don't taste good. They also consider eating healthy as unsatisfying in comparison to junk food. And they feel like they are forced to eat as an obligation more than an enjoyable diet or lifestyle.

Better Belief: these perceptions usually only occur at the beginning of your shift to a healthier diet. CKD Chef Duane says, "You probably already eat some healthy foods, let's identify those and build a healthier meal plan around them!"

By being patient and giving it time, your palate or taste will adjust. Soon enough, you'll find them delicious and rewarding.

☹ *Bogus Barrier 2: Lack of Knowledge*

People are not motivated to adapt to a healthy diet because they don't know anything about the food they are eating. This is often caused by a lack of 'nutritional knowledge' or 'nutrition misinformation'.

Better Belief: by taking this book and still reading until this chapter, you are already getting more knowledgeable about kidney-friendly nutrition than when you started!

If you want to change your mindset or perception about healthy food, you should research well on the food's nutritional aspect. You can also seek help from your doctor or health care team and ask how exactly does a healthy diet improve your condition.

😕 *Bogus Barrier 3: Prioritization*

People lose motivation to eat healthily because they can't find time to start and they have other priorities like work or other personal interests.

Better Belief: We often forget how important our health is too. How can we earn a living if we're unhealthy or sick? How can we carry out the things we're passionate about if our health hinders us from doing so?

I'm pretty sure you know the answers to these. So make sure that your health is among your priorities!

😕 *Bogus Barrier 4: Thriftiness*

In relation to prioritization as a barrier, thriftiness is also one of the reasons why people find healthy eating extra challenging. The funny thing is, CKD Chef Duane will be the first to tell you that...

..."healthy eating has to be expensive" is a MYTH.

Better Belief: sure, you will have to be more conscious about your food choices and expenses. But by doing so, you can actually discover healthier, cheaper options. For example, when comparing price per ounce at Kroger's: Beef Shaved Steak is

$0.43 but a healthier substitute like White Mushroom is only $0.24, which is almost half-priced. Beans and rice are less expensive than purchasing meat, too. And guess what, fresh fruit for your sweet fix is not only healthier, they are less expensive than buying pre-made dessert!

On a more basic level, you also need to realize that it's an investment in how you're going to spend the rest of your life. The more resources and care you put in deciding what to eat, the healthier you'll be in the long run and the less you'll end up spending for hospitalizations and healthcare.

Mental Health Journey of a CKD Patient

Linda, a vibrant woman in her fifties, had always treated life as a grand adventure until she was diagnosed with Chronic Kidney Disease (CKD). Her world seemed to shrink, and she grappled with a rush of unwelcome emotions.

She felt shocked and scared at first, the word "chronic" echoing in her mind. But Linda had always been a fighter, so she gathered her strength and embarked on this new, unexpected journey.

Dealing with CKD was challenging. Sometimes, the fatigue was overwhelming, and her radiant smile would waver. But she found solace in her beloved garden, tending to her roses and marigolds, finding peace in their blooms.

On days when the physical discomfort mounted, she turned to her close-knit book club members. Their laughter, shared stories, and words of encouragement were her balm, a sweet reminder that she was not alone.

Linda also sought professional help, speaking to a psychologist who specialized in chronic illnesses. Her therapist taught her coping mechanisms and ways to reframe her thoughts, which played an effective role in managing her anxiety.

She also joined a support group for CKD patients. Sharing experiences, fears, and small victories with those who truly understood what she was going through was profoundly comforting.

Through the highs and lows of her CKD journey, Linda realized that it's okay to be vulnerable and seek help. She learned to listen to her body and mind, to take one day at a time, and to cherish the love and support that surrounded her. She acknowledged the struggle, but refused to let it define her. And in her resilience, she found a new strength she never knew she had.

Strategies for Managing Stress

Techniques for Stress Reduction

Managing stress with chronic illness can be challenging, but there are multiple techniques that can help. Here are some recommendations:

1. **Mindfulness and Meditation**: Mindfulness is about staying present and focusing on the moment. It helps to reduce stress by preventing overthinking about past or future worries. Meditation is one way to practice mindfulness.
2. **Exercise**: Regular physical activity can boost your mood, help you sleep better, and decrease tension. It's important to consult with your doctor about suitable exercises for your condition.

3. **Social Support**: Staying connected with friends and family, joining support groups, or speaking with a mental health professional can provide emotional relief.
4. **Healthy Eating:** Certain foods can influence the body's stress response. Maintain a balanced diet with plenty of fruits, vegetables, lean proteins, and whole grains.
5. **Relaxation Techniques**: Techniques like deep breathing, progressive muscle relaxation, and yoga can reduce stress.
6. **Cognitive Behavioral Therapy (CBT)**: CBT can help you manage stress by changing negative thought patterns and developing coping strategies.

Implementing a Daily Stress-Management Routine

Implementing a daily stress-management routine is a key step in handling stress effectively. Here are some strategies you can use:

Start Your Day With Mindfulness

Spend a few minutes each morning practicing mindfulness or meditation. This can be as simple as focusing on your breath, savoring your morning coffee, or doing a guided meditation using an app like Headspace (https://www.headspace.com/) or Calm (https://www.calm.com/).

Regular Exercise

Incorporate physical activity into your daily routine. This could be a morning walk, yoga, swimming, or any exercise you enjoy. Remember to consult with a healthcare professional about what's suitable for you.

Balanced Diet

I cannot stress enough that you should ensure your meals are nutritious and balanced. Poor nutrition can exacerbate feelings of stress, while a healthy diet can boost your mood and energy levels.

Take Regular Breaks

Breaks, especially ones where you move around, can help regain focus and reduce stress during the day.

Practice Deep Breathing or Progressive Muscle Relaxation

These exercises can be done almost anywhere to help reduce immediate feelings of stress.

Connect with Others

Spend time each day connecting with loved ones, either in person, over the phone, or through video calls.

Prioritize Sleep

Good sleep hygiene is crucial for stress management. Try to have a consistent sleep schedule, and make your sleep environment as comfortable as possible.

End Your Day with Reflection

Journaling or quiet reflection can help process the events of the day, fostering gratitude and helping identify stressors.

Professional Support

If stress becomes overwhelming, consider seeking help from a mental health professional. They can provide strategies tailored to your specific needs.

Remember, different strategies work better for different people, so it's important to experiment and find what works best for you.

Chapter 9:
The Importance of Sleep in CKD Management

Understanding a your sleep patterns can provide valuable insights into your overall wellbeing and the management of Chronic Kidney Disease. I'd like you to do a quick assessment of your own sleep patterns by answering the following questions before proceeding in this chapter:

1. What time do you usually go to bed and wake up?

    _____

    This can help establish your natural sleep-wake cycle.

2. How long does it take you to fall asleep once you're in bed? _____

    Difficulty falling asleep can be a sign of insomnia.

3. Do you wake up during the night?

    _____

4. If so, how often and for how long?

    _____

    Frequent awakenings could indicate a sleep disorder.

5. Do you feel refreshed upon waking up in the morning?

    _____

    Feeling tired even after a full night's rest could indicate poor sleep quality.

6. Do you snore or has anyone ever told you that you stop breathing during sleep? _____

These might be signs of sleep apnea, which is common in CKD patients.

7. Do you experience restless legs or any other discomfort that prevents you from falling asleep?

_____

Restless legs syndrome is also common in CKD patients.

8. Do you nap during the day?

_____

9. How often and for how long?

_____

Daytime sleepiness can disrupt the sleep-wake cycle.

10. Do you consume caffeine or alcohol, and when?

_____

These substances can interfere with sleep.

11. Do you use any electronic devices (e.g., smartphones, laptops) in bed? _____

The light emitted from these devices can interfere with circadian rhythms.

12. What is your bedtime routine?

_____

A consistent routine can help signal the body that it's time to sleep.

Remember, these questions are a starting point. It would also be helpful to share these answers with your healthcare team, especially if you are experiencing some discomfort and abnormalities in your sleep.

Understanding Sleep and CKD

The Role of Sleep in Health

Sleep disorders are common in patients with CKD, including sleep apnea, insomnia, restless leg syndrome, and others. These disorders can increase the risk of high blood pressure, cardiovascular disease, and exacerbate kidney damage, all of which can further compromise kidney function.

In a study published in 2019, it was found that poor sleep quality was associated with faster CKD progression. The researchers suggested that sleep disturbances could be an overlooked factor contributing to the progression of kidney disease in these patients.

Additionally, a review article from 2020 discussed the complex relationship between CKD and sleep disorders. The authors suggested that effectively managing sleep problems could help slow the progression of kidney disease, reduce symptoms, and improve the overall quality of life for these patients.

Therefore, proper sleep management should be integrated into your comprehensive care plan as an individual with CKD. This can include lifestyle modifications, cognitive-behavioral therapy for insomnia, and treatment for specific sleep disorders.

However, it's important to note that the relationship between sleep and CKD is complex and multifactorial. Future research is needed to further understand this relationship, and to develop specific sleep interventions that can help slow the progression of CKD.

Sleep-Friendly Environment

While understanding the relationship between sleep and CKD could still be considered somewhat controversial, creating a sleep-friendly environment can be beneficial for a Chronic Kidney Disease (CKD) patient as good quality sleep can help manage stress levels and overall health. Here are some tips:

Maintain a Comfortable Sleep Environment.

Your bedroom should be quiet, dark, and cool for optimal sleep. Consider using earplugs, eye shades, or white noise machines if necessary.

Invest in a Good Quality Mattress and Pillows

These should support your body well and help prevent aches and pains that could disrupt your sleep.

Limit Light Exposure

Exposure to light stimulates alertness. Consider using heavy curtains or an eye mask to block out light. Limit screen time before bed as the blue light from screens can interfere with your body's natural sleep-wake cycle.

Regulate Your Room Temperature

A cooler room often promotes better sleep. The recommended temperature is usually around 65 degrees Fahrenheit (18.3 degrees Celsius), but it can vary per individual.

Manage Noise Levels

If you can't control the noise level outside your room, consider using a fan or a white noise machine to drown out disturbing sounds.

Keep Your Room Clean

A clean, decluttered room can help create a calm environment conducive to sleep.

Limit Bedroom Activities

Reserve your bed for sleep and intimacy only. This strengthens the mental association between your bedroom and sleep.

Consider Aromatherapy

Some people find scents like lavender and chamomile soothing and conducive to sleep. However, be sure to check that you are not allergic to these scents.

When to Seek Help for Sleep Problems

However, when these sleep problems are already causing a myriad of other inconveniences, not to mention hastening the progression of your CKD, you should consider seeking professional help for sleep problems in the following situations:

Persistent Insomnia

If you consistently have trouble falling asleep, staying asleep, or if you wake up too early and cannot get back to sleep.

Excessive Daytime Sleepiness

If you often feel excessively tired or sleepy during the day, even after a full night's sleep.

Snoring or Breathing Pauses During Sleep

Loud snoring that is followed by periods of silence and gasping could indicate sleep apnea, a condition common in CKD patients.

Restless Legs Syndrome (RLS)

If you often have an irresistible urge to move your legs while resting, particularly in the evenings.

Unrefreshing Sleep

If you regularly wake up feeling unrefreshed, even after sleeping for a sufficient number of hours.

Difficulty Adapting to a Dialysis Schedule

If you're on dialysis and are having trouble adjusting your sleep schedule.

Impact on Quality of Life

If sleep problems are causing significant distress or are interfering with your daily life.

Remember, sleep problems can be a symptom of underlying issues, some of which may be related to CKD or its treatments. Therefore, it's crucial to discuss any sleep issues with your healthcare provider so they can guide you on the best course of action.

Results of Improved Sleep Patterns

Though sometimes regarded with little attention, I have decided to really dedicate a chapter on this topic on quality sleep. I personally believe that it plays a significant role in the overall management of Chronic Kidney Disease (CKD) and contributes to a better quality of life. My belief springs from these facts and I genuinely believe that each patient should benefit from them:

1. **Improved Physical Health**. Adequate sleep allows the body to rest and repair. It supports the functioning of the immune system and helps manage CKD-related symptoms such as fatigue and weakness.

2. **Better Mental Health**. Good sleep can enhance mood and emotional regulation, reducing the risk of depression and anxiety, which are often prevalent in CKD patients.

3. **Enhanced Cognitive Function**. Quality sleep contributes to better cognition, including improved memory, attention, and problem-solving skills. This can help patients manage their treatment plans more effectively.

4. **Chronic Disease Management**. Sleep disorders are common in CKD patients and can worsen the disease's progression. Managing these sleep disorders, such as sleep apnea and insomnia, can therefore aid in CKD management.

5. **Improved Quality of Life.** Overall, getting a good night's sleep can enhance a patient's well-being and quality of life, making it easier for them to cope with the challenges of managing a chronic illness like CKD.

With your self-assesment at the beginning of this chapter, and with some introspection on the roles and significance of sleep for your CKD, I would need you to include this in your next discussions with your healthcare provider who can guide you on the best strategies or treatments to improve your sleep quality and thereby affecting your overall health.

Chapter 10:

Medication and Dietary Supplements

Managing Chronic Kidney Disease (CKD) with medication and diet is akin to steering a ship through stormy seas. Medication is the compass, providing precise direction and control, actively correcting course when the waves of disease symptoms grow too wild. A well-balanced diet, on the other hand, is the anchor, offering stability and resistance against the storm. It reinforces the ship's structure, preventing further deterioration from the relentless waves. Both are pivotal in the journey. The compass alone cannot prevent the ship from taking on water, while the anchor alone cannot guide the ship to calm seas. Only together, with medication and diet, can they navigate successfully through the storm of CKD, ensuring a safe and stable voyage.

Understanding the Importance of Medication

I am really hesitant to include this chapter on medications, not because I don't believe in them, but because I would really want this discussed to you by your doctor. However, I am also compelled to talk about the importance of medication for Chronic Kidney Disease to truly provide you with a holistic knowledge of your condition. The goal at the end of this chapter is for you to be able to identify and list down all the medications that you are taking for your kidney condition so that we will know if you are aware of what you're taking.

So before we continue, a word of warning. Doctors and pharmacists have spent a long time studying to learn when to prescribe what medications. When you have a kidney disease and are taking multiple different medications, there is a risk of side effects. This is why you should always consult with your doctor before you stop, start, or change the dosage of your medication.

If you have CKD, diabetes, or high blood pressure, you should take certain steps to protect your kidneys from harm. Your doctors can prescribe medications to help slow down the worsening of your kidneys, and prevent the complications that come from it, such as stroke or heart attack.

There are 3 factors that could help decide whether to reduce your blood pressure levels especially when you're diagnosed with CKD:

- How high your blood pressure is, especially if left untreated,
- If you have diabetes, and
- How much protein is in your urine *(albumin level)*.

A person with a normal blood pressure who doesn't have any other problems like diabetes or protein in the urine can get by without using any blood pressure medications. However, if you have those factors listed above, you are most likely to be advised to have treatment with Angiotensin-Converting Enzyme Inhibitor (ACE Inhibitor) or Angiotensin Receptor Blockers (ARBs, also known as sartans).

Let's find out which ones you have been prescribed...

ACE Inhibitors have names that end in -pril such as:

- Captopril (Capoten)
- Enalapril (Vasotec)
- Fosinopril (Monopril)
- Lisinopril (Prinivil, Zestril)
- and Ramipril (Altace)

And ARBs have names that end in -sartan such as:

- Azilsartan (Edarbi)
- Eprosartan (Teveten)
- Irbesartan (Avapro)
- Losartan (Cozaar)
- Olmesartan (Benicar)
- Valsartan (Diovan)

These are two types of blood pressure medications that are often prescribed to kidney patients to help slow down the loss of kidney function, delay kidney failure, and lower the amount of protein in your urine.

The Institute for Quality and Efficiency in Health Care posts that in a review of 119 studies involving over 64,000 participants with advanced kidney disease, ACE Inhibitors and ARBs offer several advantages compared with other blood-pressure-lowering medications (like beta blockers).

ACE inhibitors or ARBs were more effective at reducing the risk of complete kidney failure. They also reduce the risk of cardiovascular diseases such as heart attacks or strokes. There are other medications that can help prevent Stage 5 Kidney Disease, such as antihypertensive agents, diuretics (water tablets), and statins (cholesterol-lowering medication).

However, a person with CKD should avoid Motrin/Ibuprofen because it can cause Tubulointerstitial Nephritis – a disorder in which part of the kidneys become swollen, causing problems with the way your kidneys work.

Practical Things About Prescriptions

If the blood pressure medications will help my kidneys, why do I have to be extra careful?

Yes, taking blood pressure medicines will help protect your kidneys. But there are certain situations, such as when you're dehydrated from diarrhea or the flu when you need to pay attention to your blood pressure. Dehydration can lower OR raise your blood pressure! In either scenario, your kidneys might not be able to properly filter.

The best person to give you advice is your nephrologist. Make sure to ask them a list of symptoms or warning signs you need to be aware of for your specific medical situation.

But how about supplements? Will they help?

It's still highly questionable whether over-the-counter dietary, herbal and other natural supplements can help people diagnosed with CKD. Muscle-building supplements such as whey protein powders or creatinine supplements can also affect your lab results for kidney health numbers. If possible, avoid most herbal supplements unless approved by your nephrologist and dietitian.

It's important that you mention taking any supplements or alternative medicine.

What should I do at the pharmacy?

The next time you pick up your prescription or buy an over-the-counter medicine or supplement, ask your pharmacist how the product may affect your kidneys and how it will react with the other medicines that you're taking.

Fill your prescriptions at only one pharmacy or at least a pharmacy chain so that your pharmacist can carefully monitor your medicines and supplements. It can be helpful to bring a print-out with a list of all your prescriptions, you can ask for one at your doctor's office.

What should I do at my doctor's or dietitian's office?

Be sure to keep an up-to-date list of your prescribed medicines and supplements with you for your appointment. If possible, you can bring all your medicine bottles with you as well.

When CKD Chef Duane was still on medications, he always carried his list with him. If he ever had an emergency or questions about medications, his list was always in his wallet.

What should I remember about Over-The-Counter (OTC) medicines?

If you take over-the-counter medicines for headaches, pain, fever, or even colds, you may be taking non-steroidal anti-inflammatory drugs (NSAIDs), such as ibuprofen and motrin. As mentioned above, these drugs may be dangerous to your kidneys.

Here is a short list of the most common OTC medicines to be careful of:

PROBLEM	MEDICATION	BRAND NAMES
Pain	**Ibuprofen**	Advil, Motrin
Pain/Swelling	**Naproxen**	Naprosyn, Aleve
Constipation	**Sodium Phosphorous solutions**	Fleets enemas
Constipation	**Magnesium citrate**	MagCitrate

Here are OTC medicines you MAY take (unless advised by your physician):

PROBLEM	MEDICATION	BRAND NAMES
Cough	**Dextromethorphan**	Delsym
	Guaifenesin	Robitussin
Congestion (Sedating)	**Diphenhydramine**	Benadryl
	Chlorpheniramine	Chlor-Trimeton
Heartburn	**Famotidine**	Pepcid
Nausea/Motion Sickness (Sedating)	**Dimenhydrinate**	Dramamine
Gas and Bloating	**Simethicone**	Gas-X
	Alpha-D-Galactosidase	Beano
· Diarrhea	**Loperamide**	Imodium
Constipation	**Docusate Sodium**	Colace
	Lactulose	Enulose
Insomnia	**Diphenhydramine**	Benadryl
	Acetaminophen PM	Tylenol PM

Reference: BIDMC Welcome Booklet for CKD Patients

Again, be sure to ask your doctors if the OTC medicines you are taking are safe to use with your current prescribed CKD medicines.

***What is self-medication? Is that something
I need to worry about?***

Self-medication is when you take medicine because you or another person (who is not a doctor) think it can help with your condition. It is normal for some people. It is just something they prefer to do rather than going to the doctor which can be time-consuming and expensive. However, what they don't realize is that opting for self-medication makes us prone to allergies or even drug dependence. Or it can have the opposite effect, such as in the case of medical cannabis where kidneys become worse *faster*.

Also, remember it is your doctor's job to make sure that you get the right medical treatment. Every doctor would prefer that you call them with a question about your medication, than that you make a mistake that damages your kidneys.

Unfortunately, there is very little or almost no awareness about the disadvantages of self-medication. Taking pills may get us instant relief but it does not mean we are free from the side effects. Oftentimes, a patient may be under-prescribed medication for a different health issue, and self-medicating may lead to unfortunate reactions.

Why? Because one drug may react differently when consumed with another prescribed drug. In rare cases, this can even lead to death. Which is why <u>consulting a doctor is very important</u>.

Which leads me to my next question...

Do you keep track of your prescribed medications?

If yes, I want you to list them all down, especially if you have been prescribed a blood pressure drug. Once you've got that list ready, I need you to send them over along with the hurdles you experience when taking them to your doctor and dietitian.

Chapter 11:
Staying Motivated and Dealing with Setbacks

We are finally at the end of the book, and I can't express enough how proud I am of you for devoting your time and putting effort into having the best possible health while battling with CKD.

After reading this book is the time when you actually will start the real journey. And let me tell you, it's not always going to be easy. You will deal with some minor or even major setbacks, and them some more along the way.

But I trust that we were able to build a solid foundation and that in going through this journey, you have the right tools to break through each barrier that comes along your way. When the tools don't work anymore, all you need to do is sharpen your tools by going back and flipping through the pages of this book.

And I don't want to close this by not leaving one more secret weapon that will help you to be always on guard and ready for the battle that's ahead.

Ask For Help: Let's Overcome Those Support Setbacks

Now the question is: what are the different Support Setbacks that most patients face when trying to ask for help? More importantly, what can you do to overcome them? Let's find out!

🚫 Support Setback 1: Stigma

Did you ever feel like you were embarrassed about your condition? And this made it harder for you to tell people, especially your doctor, about it?

Stigma is common among patients with chronic diseases. Recent studies show that the representations of illness associated with CKD gave rise to social stigma among some diagnosed patients. This is particularly true with patients who are also experiencing depression upon knowing they are diagnosed with CKD.

And we understand that. Anyone could feel the same. It takes a lot of heart and courage to deal with the mental health challenges that come along with CKD. If you've come this far, then you're doing great and we're here to support you all the way through.

But if you have been struggling with opening up, don't worry, we're here to help and guide you.

So to overcome this barrier, you simply need to open up slowly. Don't rush it. Start sharing your thoughts and feelings with your closest circle like your family and friends first.

Once you do that, you'll be able to create your first line of support. This is important because if you establish your support system with people you're comfortable with, everything that comes next will be a lot easier.

Most of the time, they would also encourage you to open up more to someone else. Eventually, you'll feel better and more confident talking to your doctor if you have your family right beside you.

Always remember that you're not alone and you don't need to do this all by yourself.

⊘ Support Setback 2: Lack of Trust

You probably had some doubts about your doctor which made it harder for you to talk to him or her about your condition. And since we're talking about your health here, it's definitely understandable and even normal to be skeptical at first.

But the problem comes if this persists for way too long. The only way your healthcare team can help you is if you meet them halfway.

According to Dr. Carlos A. Pellegrini, the Chief Medical Officer for University of Washington Medicine and a Professor in the Department of Surgery,

"Trust is the keystone of the physician-patient relationship."

Without trust, reaching out will be too difficult. So if you're struggling with trusting your healthcare team, what should you do?

Again, you need to take things slowly. Build a relationship with them. For starters, don't stop at being a care recipient. Play an active role in your own health by asking them about your condition. Ask them about your medications. And maybe from time to time, ask them about their day too. Let yourself be educated by them.

After some time, you won't even notice it but you're already going with the flow. Just like good friendships, you'll eventually trust them enough to help you out on your road to recovery – or even let them be a significant part of your life.

⃠ Support Setback 3: Hopelessness

"What's the point of asking for help when it's hopeless?"

"It's too late. No one can help me."

"There's just no way out of this."

A lot of patients also struggle to seek help because of feelings of hopelessness. You've probably had moments like these too, without a doubt. And for you to be able to seek help properly, you need to overcome these feelings.

One way to overcome hopelessness is to look for motivations. Ask yourself.

What wakes you up in the morning?

What makes you happy?

What makes you want to live?

Sometimes, looking for a single but strong motivation is all it takes to keep you hopeful and going on again.

You can also look forward to something new every day--- whether that's a new hobby, a new skill or talent, or doing something you've never done before.

And it may be a cliche, but it will always stand true: don't ever stop hoping for a better tomorrow.

Once you have that motivation back, asking for help will be so much easier. And you'll be surprised by how much it will change your overall lifestyle!

So remember, to overcome these barriers: take it slow, build relationships, be educated, be motivated, and look forward to a great future just ahead of you.

3 Motivation Movers

It's one thing to be motivated, but it's another thing to keep yourself motivated. So let's lay down a few things you can do to keep the momentum for healthy eating up and running.

🏆 Motivation Mover 1: Start with your WHYs

If you find yourself lost while looking for an ounce of motivation, just ask your whys:

"Why should I lessen my sodium intake?"

"Why should I strive to do better?"

"Why did I do my best to make it this far in my health goals?"

Asking yourself these questions and finding out the reasons behind everything you do will help you direct yourself to your health goals. This will help you establish what you really want to do and accomplish.

And more often than not, directions can help you in reaching or achieving the outcomes you want.

🏆 Motivation Mover 2: Make it enjoyable

In everything that you do to change or improve your lifestyle, in this particular case, your diet or food/nutrient intake, always find a way to make it enjoyable.

You can do this in a lot of ways too! You can look for healthy and creative recipes online that can suit your health needs or you can try to learn something new every day---whether that's a new recipe or new information about your health by reading scientific articles or asking help from your doctor.

As long as you find your lifestyle enjoyable, you'll have less worrying to do in keeping yourself motivated.

🏆 Motivation Mover 3: Never hesitate to ask for help or support

Slip-ups will occur occasionally along the way and it's fine. Sometimes, it might get lonely as well – it's as if you're carrying everything on your own. But this is simply not true. You have your doctor, healthcare team, friends, and family to help you every step of the way.

Surround yourself with people you care about and you don't have to do things alone.

If you ever find yourself losing motivation and you feel like you can't pull yourself together on your own, remember that you have people around you who will never think twice before helping you. It's always more motivational and encouraging to keep going on if you know that you will always have company around no matter what.

Remember, your mental health is just as important as your physical health. For you to improve your overall health, these two aspects should work together.

While what we've discussed are just a few of the things you can do to strengthen your motivation, and consequently your mental health, they're a great way to start. So as long as you keep your mental health in check, your will and motivation to make changes in your lifestyle and to do better will never burn out.

Now, all throughout this book, we've established the undeniable fact that making changes to your lifestyle (and ultimately adapting to them) can require a tremendous amount of work and effort from your end. This can make your nutritional or diet adaptation (along with your overall behavior and habits relevant to your health) quite challenging and overwhelming.

But we've also established that this takes time and a few slip-ups along the way are to be expected – and these are all fine!

Eventually, though, you'll get the hang of it. Especially when you know that making even the littlest changes to your diet, your workout, and your overall daily routines, as a significant part of managing your own health, could go a long way in the future. In fact, you probably are now too! And you're definitely taking big steps towards your recovery.

At some point, however, if we were to look through a long-term prospect, you might start to realize and ask yourself the question: *how will you know if the self-management practices you've been carrying out are actually working?*

Of course, one way to check your progress is to consult your healthcare team. This is more particularly applicable to your health's biophysical aspect.

Through a series of medical tests, your doctor can make an assessment and conclude whether or not the changes and adaptations you're making in your lifestyle have significantly contributed to your health improvement.

But since self-management is taking charge of your own health, it's important for you to monitor your condition along with the progress you're making along the way as well.

Strategies to Overcome Setbacks

Ultimately, we all want to have more control over our health. That's what we've always been aiming for since day one – laying out the cards in the table that can help you win in the end. But we also want to go beyond that. It's one thing to change your lifestyle and recover; keeping up with it, however, is another.

And so we want to bring about a significant effect on your health that doesn't stop at your recovery. We'll do this by presenting you two simple self-assessment measures you can use that can determine if you're taking the right steps towards adapting, managing your own health, and improving your overall lifestyle.

Being able to motivate yourself

Reinforcement theories under social psychology suggest that people can devise reinforcements (rewards or things that can encourage them to carry out or maintain good habits) to help them achieve their desired outcomes.

Children, for example, are given treats or toys if they do a good job at something (let's say, winning a quiz bee or acing an exam). While this seems to be a usual thing we see in every pre-school environment we've been to, it can motivate kids to always do their best and it can carry on such a habit until they grow up.

Positive reinforcements, however, don't only work among kids. In low-key but also profound ways, it affects us too! Doing a great job at work can give us recognition from our workmates and even a promotion which can inspire us to do better. A hearty and healthy meal with good company after finishing a project can drive us to continue the hard work. And simply hearing words of encouragement from our loved ones can keep us going.

As you can see, a lot of positive reinforcements are rooted in socially based drives – we want companionship, we want to be accepted, and well, who doesn't want to be loved?

It's not that bad to look for motivation from other people too. But there will be times when you need to work on it on your own, especially in cases where others just can't seem to give you the motivation or support you need. It's part of taking charge of your own health.

You need to have your own set of personal-based motivations. You need to have control over what keeps you going. It's through this that you can truly drive yourself to always do your best.

This won't be easy the first time too because a lot of us usually rely on the support of others. But once you gain such strong control over this dynamic in your life, I'm confident that you will always be able to manage your health and maintain a healthy lifestyle under any circumstances.

Dealing with failures appropriately (Stress Management)

Sometimes, people may find themselves in more difficult situations than others when dealing with failures. Of course, feeling down for the first few missteps is normal. The problem arises, however, if you stop dealing with them maturely or realistically and just let your defeat consume you.

This is more especially common among patients who were just diagnosed with a chronic condition thinking that they need to immediately adjust their lifestyle in order to cope with it.

I'm sure that the pressure you've been feeling back then might be relatively tenser than the stress you've dealt with after a few weeks or months of your adjustments. Upon knowing about your condition, you surely had your thoughts rushing in all together.

And you've probably only thought about your recovery and how to get there as fast as you can.

Most people never really give so much thought about failing, because who would want to fail in the first place? We just want to skip that part and then take the shorter route---the route without barriers. The thing though, is that it's by accepting the inevitable fact that you will certainly face a few failures, missteps, and slip-ups that can you truly deal with them. If you fed yourself with the idea that everything will be perfect in your self-improvement progress, you will only end up discouraged once you stumble upon one and fail to solve it.

You need to keep in mind that failures are part of our growth and more often than not, they have shaped some of our good qualities as individuals.

Again, to feel a bit down from a failure is normal. What matters, however, are the things that you do to overcome them. Don't let it drown you.

You'll find it easier to adapt to any lifestyle change if you learn how to appropriately deal with failures.

Now, these are just two self-assessment measures you can use to evaluate your self-improvement. But they could tell significant information about your overall progress.

Sometimes, self-perception could get tricky as well because your self-evaluation greatly rests on your own judgment. You might get to a point where you want to drop your progress even though you've barely made compelling changes and adjustments to your lifestyle because it's just simply draining and overwhelming. You might think you've failed. But as we've said earlier, it's only by recognizing the failures you'll inevitably come across somewhere along the way (coupled with your own will to compensate for your shortcomings) that can you genuinely address and win your struggles.

So just remember to try and try. Rest for a while but always pick up where you left off and continue again. And be as objective as you can when assessing yourself.

I would love to hear from you!

It's through your support and reviews that my book is able to reach other Chronic Kidney Disease patients who are still struggling to figure out how they could take a proactive approach in managing their CKD. Please take 60 seconds to kindly leave a review on Amazon. Please scan the QR code below, alternatively, you may use the link provided in your Amazon order.

Please follow these simple steps to rate/review my book:

1. Open the camera on your phone

2. Hover it over the QR code below

3. You may also type this link on your phone or browser: **https://go.renaltracker.com/bookreview**

4. Rate/Review my book

I appreciate you taking the time, your review will surely make a difference.

Thank you!

Janeth Kingston

Conclusion

As we navigate the journey of life, living with Chronic Kidney Disease (CKD) presents its own unique challenges. Over the years I've spent as a kidney nurse, I have been committed to guiding and supporting you through this journey. This book has been a part of that commitment, emphasizing the crucial role of diet and nutrition in managing CKD.

Food is not just for enjoyment; it's a primary source of fuel for our bodies. It helps build our cells, powers our activities and strengthens our immune systems. In the context of CKD, proper nutrition can help control symptoms, slow the progression of the disease, and significantly improve the quality of life. It's not a cure, but it's a powerful strategy that you have control over every day.

It's important to remember that dietary needs for CKD vary greatly from person to person. Each individual's situation is unique, influenced by disease stage, other health conditions, and personal preferences. That's why it's essential to consult with your doctor and work with a nutritionist or dietitian. Their expertise can help you tailor a diet plan that aligns with your health needs and accommodates your lifestyle and tastes.

These professionals are knowledgeable guides who can help you navigate the sometimes complex world of nutrition. They can break down the latest research, debunk common myths, and provide practical and personalized advice. They can help you understand why certain foods need to be limited, why others should be encouraged, and how to strike a balance between maintaining a healthy diet and enjoying your meals.

As we conclude this book, please know that this is not the end of our journey together. Through my other books focused on CKD, I will continue to provide you with the latest and most relevant information. Living with CKD can be challenging, but with the right guidance, a well-balanced diet, and an openness to learning, you can lead a fulfilling life.

Remember, CKD is a part of your life, but it doesn't define who you are. You have the ability to make choices, ask questions, and seek support. Your engagement is as important as the guidance you receive.

So, let's not view this as a goodbye, but rather a pause in our ongoing conversation. I look forward to our continued dialogue and shared learning. Until we meet again in the pages of another book, take care, stay curious, and continue to prioritize your health and nutrition.

DATE & DAY_____   (S)(M)(T)(W)(T)(F)(S)

- BLOOD PRESSURE
- COFFEE (svgs)
- FRUITS (svgs)
- VEGGIES (svgs)
- CIGARETTES

- WAKE UP TIME:
- SLEEP (hrs)
- WATER ▢▢▢▢▢▢▢
- EXERCISE(s) DONE
  _____
  _____

Positive Confession
_____
_____

I am Thankful for
_____
_____

Daily Limits
PROTEIN (G) _____ POTASSIUM (MG) _____ PHOSPHORUS (MG) _____ SODIUM (MG) _____

	FOOD	PROTEIN	POTASSIUM	PHOS.	SODIUM	CALORIES
BREAKFAST:						
	SUBTOTAL					
LUNCH:						
	SUBTOTAL					
DINNER:						
	SUBTOTAL					

Medications and Supplements
_____
_____
_____
_____

Symptom Tracker

Swelling/Edema	Fatigue	Nausea	Vomiting
Shortness of breath	Itching	Muscle Cramps	Poor Sleep

Other Symptoms:
_____

References

Stirring the Pot: Can Dietary Modification Alleviate the Burden of CKD? Snelson et. al. https://www.mdpi.com/2072-6643/9/3/265

Importance of Age and Metabolism in CKD Dieting

- National Institute on Aging - Sarcopenia with Aging - https://www.nia.nih.gov/health/sarcopenia-loss-muscle-mass-strength-and-function-aging

Nutritional Needs of the 50+ Age Group

National Institute on Aging - Choosing Healthy Meals As You Get Older

Harvard Health Publishing - Special Nutrient Needs of Older Adults

Mayo Clinic - Dietary fiber: Essential for a healthy diet

Oregon State University - Micronutrient Information Center: Vitamin B12

National Institutes of Health Office of Dietary Supplements - Vitamin D

National Institutes of Health Office of Dietary Supplements - Potassium

American Heart Association - Shaking the Salt Habit to Lower High Blood Pressure

CDC - Nutrition for Older Adults

Impact of Food on your Kidneys

- [National Kidney Foundation: 6 Harmful Things for your Kidneys] (https://www.kidney.org/atoz/content/sixstepshealthprimer)

- [American Kidney Fund: Kidney-friendly diet for CKD] (https://www.kidneyfund.org/kidney-disease/chronic-kidney-disease-ckd/kidney-friendly-diet-for-ckd.html)

- [Mayo Clinic: Chronic kidney disease] (https://www.mayoclinic.org/diseases-conditions/chronic-kidney-disease/symptoms-causes/syc-20354521)

The Diet and Haemodialysis Dyad: Three Eras, Four Open Questions and Four Paradoxes. A Narrative Review, Towards a Personalized, Patient-Centered Approach

- https://www.mdpi.com/2072-6643/9/4/372

Vegetarian Diet in Chronic Kidney Disease—A Friend or Foe

- https://www.mdpi.com/2072-6643/9/4/374

ROLE OF MACRONUTRIENT AND MICRONUTRIENT IN CKD

- [National Kidney Foundation: Protein and Chronic Kidney Disease](https://www.kidney.org/atoz/content/protein)

- [National Kidney Foundation: Carbohydrates and Chronic Kidney Disease](https://www.kidney.org/atoz/content/carbs)

- [National Kidney Foundation: Fats and Chronic Kidney Disease](https://www.kidney.org/atoz/content/fats)

- [National Kidney Foundation: Potassium and Chronic Kidney Disease](https://www.kidney.org/atoz/content/potassium)

- [National Kidney Foundation: Phosphorus and Your CKD Diet](https://www.kidney.org/atoz/content/phosphorus)

- [National Kidney Foundation: Vitamin D and Chronic Kidney Disease](https://www.kidney.org/atoz/content/vitaminD)

IMPORTANCE OF INDIVIDUAL DIETARY REQUIREMENTS

[National Kidney Foundation: Nutrition and Chronic Kidney Disease]

(https://www.kidney.org/atoz/content/nutrichronic)

IMPORTANCE OF HYDRATION AND FLUID RESTRICTION IN CKD

- [National Kidney Foundation: High Blood Pressure and Chronic Kidney Disease] (https://www.kidney.org/atoz/content/highblood)

- [National Kidney Foundation: Swelling and Chronic Kidney Disease] (https://www.kidney.org/atoz/content/swelling)

- [National Kidney Foundation: Shortness of Breath and Chronic Kidney Disease] (https://www.kidney.org/atoz/content/shortness-breath-and-chronic-kidney-disease)

- [National Kidney Foundation: Dehydration and Kidney Disease] (https://www.kidney.org/newsletter/can-dehydration-affect-your-kidneys)

- [National Kidney Foundation: What Do You Mean I Can't Have a Fresca?] (https://www.kidney.org/blog/kidney-diet-tips/kidney-diet-tips-what-do-you-mean-I-cant-have-fresca)

CHOOSING THE RIGHT BEVERAGE IN CKD

- [National Kidney Foundation: Potassium and Your CKD Diet] (https://www.kidney.org/atoz/content/potassium)

- [National Kidney Foundation: Phosphorus and Your CKD Diet] (https://www.kidney.org/atoz/content/phosphorus)

- [National Kidney Foundation: Alcohol and Chronic Kidney Disease] (https://www.kidney.org/atoz/content/alcohol)

- [National Kidney Foundation: Sodium and Your CKD Diet] (https://www.kidney.org/atoz/content/sodiumckd)

STATISTICS ON PPPS

- [American Journal of Physiology-Renal Physiology: High salt intake and chronic kidney disease] (https://journals.physiology.org/doi/full/10.1152/ajprenal.00025.2015)

- [Cochrane Database of Systematic Reviews: Low protein diets for chronic kidney disease in non diabetic adults] (https://www.cochranelibrary.com/cdsr/doi/10.1002/14651858.CD001892.pub3/full)

- [American Journal of Kidney Diseases: Serum Potassium Levels and Mortality in Chronic Kidney Disease] (https://www.ajkd.org/article/S0272-6386(10)01156-3/fulltext)

- [Journal of the American Society of Nephrology: Serum Phosphorus and Risk of Cardiovascular Disease, All-Cause Mortality, or Graft Failure in Kidney Transplant Recipients: An Ancillary Study of the FAVORIT Trial Cohort] (https://jasn.asnjournals.org/content/28/9/2756)

- http://i.imgur.com/DWeLkhA.png

Food Journal Guide/Sample

- https://healthiestlife4me.wordpress.com/2012/03/25/week-9-food-diary-sample/

Food Label Sample

- https://esha.com/blog/potassium-rounding-rules-on-the-2016-nutrition-facts-panel/

Food Portioning Guide

- https://www.pinterest.ph/pin/298152437809682150/

WORKING WITH A DIETITIAN

- The Academy of Nutrition and Dietetics (www.eatright.org), The National Kidney Foundation (www.kidney.org),

STRATEGIES FOR MANAGING STRESS

- [Mindful] (https://www.mindful.org/) and [Headspace] (https://www.headspace.com/meditation-101/what-is-meditation).

- The [Mayo Clinic]

- (https://www.mayoclinic.org/healthy-lifestyle/stress-management/in-depth/exercise-and-stress/art-20044469)

- [American Psychological Association] (http://www.apa.org/helpcenter/emotional-support).

- [Harvard Medical School]

- (https://www.health.harvard.edu/blog/nutritional-strategies-to-ease-anxiety-201604139441) website.

- [Mayo Clinic]

- (https://www.mayoclinic.org/healthy-lifestyle/stress-management/in-depth/relaxation-technique/art-20045368).

- American Psychological Association (https://www.apa.org/ptsd-guideline/patients-and-families/cognitive-behavioral).

UNDERSTANDING SLEEP AND CKD

- Masood, M., et al. (2018). Sleep Disorders and Chronic Kidney Disease. World Journal of Nephrology.

- Molnar, MZ., et al. (2019). Association of Quality of Sleep with Cognitive Decline and Risk of Incident Dementia: Reasons for Geographic and Racial Differences. Sleep.

- Roumelioti, ME., et al. (2020). Sleep Disorders and Chronic Kidney Disease. World Journal of Nephrology.

- Mayo Clinic (https://www.mayoclinic.org/diseases-conditions/insomnia/symptoms-causes/syc-20355167).

- National Kidney Foundation
  (https://www.kidney.org/atoz/content/sleep).

- National Kidney Foundation
  (https://www.kidney.org/news/ekidney/june10/SleepProblems_june 10) and [American Journal of Kidney Diseases](https://www.ajkd.org/article/S0272-6386(16)30523-8/fulltext) for more information.

UNDERSTANDING MEDICATIONS

- https://www.ncbi.nlm.nih.gov/books/NBK492989

- https://www.ncbi.nlm.nih.gov/pmc/articles/PMC4421632/#:~:text=There%20is%20less%20concern%20today,should%20avoid%20using%20this%20supplement.

- https://www.sciencedirect.com/topics/medicine-and-dentistry/self-medication

- https://www.kidneyfund.org/kidney-today/a-caution-about-self-medication-for-kidney-patients.html

Made in the USA
Las Vegas, NV
15 October 2024